SPEKTRUM
Berliner Reihe zu Gesellschaft, Wirtschaft und
Politik in Entwicklungsländern · ISSN 0176-277 X

Herausgegeben von

Prof. Dr. Volker Lühr und Prof. Dr. Manfred Schulz

Freie Universität Berlin · Institut für Soziologie
Babelsberger Straße 14-16 · 1000 Berlin 31
Telefon (0 30) 8 53 70 51 App. 271

Erscheint in unregelmäßiger Folge. Für unverlangt
zugesandte Manuskripte keine Gewähr.

SPEKTRUM

Berliner Reihe zu Gesellschaft, Wirtschaft und
Politik in Entwicklungsländern

Herausgegeben von
Prof. Dr. Volker Lühr und Prof. Dr. Manfred Schulz

Band 7

Hassan Omari Kaya

Problems of Regional Development in Tanzania

A Case Study of the Tanga Region

Verlag **breitenbach** Publishers
Saarbrücken · Fort Lauderdale 1985

CIP-Kurztitelaufnahme der Deutschen Bibliothek

Kaya, Hassan Omari:
Problems of regional development in Tanzania: a case study of the Tanga region / Hassan Omari Kaya. – Saarbrücken; Fort Lauderdale: Breitenbach, 1985.

   (Spektrum; Bd. 7)
   ISBN 3-88156-302-4
NE: GT

ISBN 3-88156-302-4

© 1985 by Verlag **breitenbach** Publishers
Memeler Straße 50, D-6600 Saarbrücken, Germany
P.O.B. 16243 Fort Lauderdale, Fla, 33318, USA

Printed by **arco**-Druck GmbH, Hallstadt

LIST OF CONTENTS

I.	INTRODUCTION	1
1.	Definition of the Problems	1
1.1	Aims of the Study	6
1.3.	Hypotheses	7
1.4.	Motivation to Undertake the Study	8
1.5.	Organisation of the Study	9
	Footnotes for Introduction	11
II.	THEORETICAL APPROACHES AND METHODOLOGY OF THE STUDY	15
2.1.	Theoretical Approaches	15
2.2.	Methodology	33
2.2.1.	Examination of Secondary Data	33
2.2.2.	Interviews	34
2.2.2.1.	Selection of Sample Sisal Plantations and Labourers	35
2.2.2.2.	Selection of Sample Villages and Households	38
2.2.2.3.	Identification of the Household	40
2.2.2.4.	Migration	42
2.2.2.5.	Employment	43
2.2.2.6.	Income/Assets	44
2.2.2.7.	Key-Persons	45
2.2.3.	Participatory Observation	46
2.4.	Summary	47
	Footnotes for Chapter Two	49

III.	THE GENERAL CHARACTERISTICS OF THE TANGA REGION	55
3.1.	Location	55
3.2.	Size and Administrative Divisions	55
3.3.	Physiography	59
3.4.	Climate	59
3.5.	Population and its structure	62
3.5.1.	Size and Distribution	63
3.5.2.	Sex-ratios and Age groups	65
3.5.3.	Tribal Groupings and their Socio-economic Structures	66
3.5.3.1.	The Zigua	67
3.5.3.1.1.	Distribution	67
3.5.3.1.2.	Economic Activities	68
3.5.3.1.3.	Housing Patterns	70
3.5.3.1.4.	Pre-Colonial Kinship Relations	71
3.5.3.1.5.	Marriage Relationships	72
3.5.3.1.6.	Division of Labour	73
3.5.3.1.7.	Religions	74
3.5.3.2.	The Shambaa	76
3.5.3.2.1.	Distribution and Economic Activities	76
3.5.3.2.2.	Traditional and 'Modern' Village Patterns	79
3.5.3.2.3.	Pre-Colonial Kinship Relations	81
3.5.3.2.3.1.	Social Differentiation	83
3.5.3.3.	Other Tribal Groups	85
3.6.	Summary	87
	Footnotes for Chapter Three	90

IV.	THE RESPONSE OF THE LOCAL PEASANTRY TO WAGE-LABOUR IN THE SISAL PLANTATIONS	95
4.1.	Theories on African Wage-labour	96
4.2.	Introduction to the Sisal Industry and the Wage-Labour Question in the Sisal Plantations	104
4.2.1.	Introduction of the Sisal Industry	104
4.2.2.	Background to the Wage Labour Problem	105
4.2.2.1.	Colonial Efforts to Solve the Labour Problems	108
4.3.	The Nationalization Policy and Characteristics of Wage Labour in the Present Sisal Plantation System	115
4.3.1.	The Nationalization Policy	115
4.3.2.	Characteristics of Wage-Labour in the Present Sisal Plantation System	116
4.3.2.1.	Categories of Employees	116
4.3.2.2.	Sex Structure	118
4.3.2.3.	Age and Education	119
4.3.2.4.	Tribal Origin of the Workers	119
4.3.2.5.	Workers' Ownership and Participation in Management	127
4.3.2.6.	Summary	134
	Foootnotes for Chapter Four	137
V.	PEASANTS VERSUS GOVERNMENT	143
5.1.	Theories on the African Peasantry	143
5.2.	Tanga Region Experience	148
5.2.1.	Background to Peasant Export-Production	148
5.2.2.	The Post-independence Peasant Agricultural Production	154

5.2.2.1.	The Transformation and Improvement Approaches	154
5.2.2.2.	Rural Development Through Socialism and Self-reliance	159
5.2.2.3.	Limitations of Ujamaa Development and New Approach in Agricultural Production	162
5.2.2.4.	A Brief Historical Background of the Post-Independence Cooperative Societies	175
5.2.2.5.	The Limitations of the Primary Cooperative Societies	181
5.2.2.6.	Agricultural Extension and Other Rural Socio-Economic Services	187
5.2.2.6.1.	Health Facilities	196
5.2.2.6.2.	Water Supply	197
5.3.	Summary	200
	Footnotes for Chapter Five	204
VI.	CONCLUSIONS	211
6.1.	Proletarianization of the Peasantry	211
6.2.	Rural Development Programmes	212
6.2.1.	Distribution of Agricultural Extension Services	213
6.2.2.	Education Services	214
6.2.3.	Health and Water Facilities	215
6.3.	Lessons Derived from the Findings	217
	BIBLIOGRAPHY	220
	APPENDIX	231

LIST OF TABLES

No.	Title	Page
2.1	The Surveyed Sisal Plantations in the Korogwe and Handeni Districts (1983)	36
2.2	The Surveyed Villages and Households in Korogwe and Handeni District (1983)	38
3.1	Administrative Districts and Divisions in the Tanga Region (1983)	57
3.2	Average Annual Rainfall in the District Towns of the Tanga Region	62
3.3	Population Density per District (1978)	64
3.4	School-age Children and Working-age Adults as Percentages of the Total Population and Sex-ratios in the Districts of the Tanga Region (1979)	66
4.1	A Comparison Between Wage-earners in 10 African Countries and 10 Industrialized Countries Surveyed by ILO in 1982	100
4.2	Percentages of the Contribution of the Sisal Industry to Total Employment in the Economy of Tanzania	114
4.3	Total Average Labour Force per Annum in Tanzania Sisal Plantation System, 1960-1980	116
4.4	Origin of the Sisal Plantation Workers in the 9 Surveyed Plantations in Korogwe and Handeni Districts	120
4.5	Duration of Current Job by Tribal Categories of the Workers in the Sisal Plantations of the Tanga Region	122
4.6	Distribution of the Workers in the Different Activities of the Sisal Plantation Surveyed in Korogwe and Handeni Districts (According to their Places of Origin)	125
5.1	The Value of Products from the Usambaras exported through the Port of Tanga in the Period 1888/89 and 1889/90 (Value in Marks)	149

No.	Title	Page
5.2	The Value of Products from the Usambaras exported through the Port of Pangani in the Period 1888/89 and 1889/90 (Value in Marks)	150
5.3	Principal Total Exports sent to Germany from German East Africa in 1911 (Value in Marks)	152
5.4	Chronological Development of 'Ujamaa Villages' in Tanzania	161
5.5	Development of Ujamaa Villages in the Tanga Region	161
5.6	Cotton Production on Ujamaa and Private Farms in the Korogwe District as Percentages of Total Production	166
5.7	Land Distribution in Two Divisions of Korogwe District (1982)	168
5.8	Land Distribution in 7 Divisions of Handeni District (1982)	168
5.9	Annual Output of Main Staple Grains in Tanzania (in Tons)	171
5.10	Official Producer Prices of Maize and Paddy (1983)	173
5.11	Family Labour Force and Man/Land Ratios on Individual Farms in the Tanga Region (1980)	174
5.12	Marketing Channels for Agricultural Crops in the Tanga Region	180
5.13	Distribution of the Existing Cooperative Societies in the Korogwe District (1983)	185
5.14	Distribution of the Existing Cooperative Societies in the Handeni District (1983)	185
5.15	Distribution of Primary Schools, Classrooms and Teachers' Houses in the Tanga Region (1982)	191
5.16	Enrolment of Adult Education in the Tanga Region (1980)	195
5.17	Comparative Distribution of Health Facilities Between Korogwe and Handeni Districts (1979)	197

ACKNOWLEDGMENTS

A study like this one which involved field-surveys could not have been possible without the cooperation of other people. I would like to mention only a few whom I have frequently called for help.

I am greatly indebted to the Otto Benecke Foundation for supporting me financially and to Prof. Dr. Manfred Schulz of the Sociology Institute (Free University Berlin-West) who has followed the preparation and the writing of the thesis stage by stage.
I am grateful to Dr. K. Hubert of the German Agency for Technical Cooperation (GTZ) in Eschborn, Frankfurt, who provided me with useful material on the activities of the Tanga Integrated Rural Development Programme (TIRDEP).
My deep gratitude should also go to Mr. Ahmad Muya of the College of Business Education in Dodoma, Tanzania, who guided me during my research surveys in the Handeni district where he comes from.
Thanks are also due to Mr. Hassan Majili, the District Party Chairman of Handeni District, and Mr. Babu, the District Development Director of Korogwe District who gave me useful ideas about the political and socio-economic situations in their respective districts and the Tanga Region at large, including their moral encouragement for me to continue with the study. Finally, I would like to express my gratitude to the University of Dar es salaam for granting me an extended study leave to do my doctorate studies abroad.

I.   INTRODUCTION

1. Definition of the Problems

An academic examination of the limitations of the socio-economic development in the rural areas of Tanzania and Africa at large is a current undertaking.[1] This includes studies on the responses of the rural people to aspects like wage-labour, land tenure, price policies and other socio-economic changes from outside their local communities.

The examination into such aspects on African studies has been retarded by:
(i)   the restriction for a long period of time in African studies to the field of anthropology, both as a means of justifying colonialism and as an emanation of the colonial ideology.[2]
(ii) the elimination of indigenous African educational institutions and a simultaneous, slow development of westernised educational institutions in Africa, resulting in a small number of African scholars capable of analysing the socio-economic problems of their own societies.
(iii) the ethnocentric attitudes of the bulk of the European and American scholars.

The colonial situation was one in which the local populations were both exposed to new goods and services and, in many cases subjected to specific government-enforced economic or labour demands, with the result that new needs were generated which could only be met by participating in the market economy. In order to fit into the pattern of the colonial economic ex-

ploitation, the colonial territory was segmented into 'subsistence'[3], export-crops, livestock, and labour supplying areas.[4]
These patterns were not static. They changed as the whole system developed. However, in certain areas over-emphasis on cash crop production led to the impoverishment of the soils.[5] Moreover, the introduction of new agricultural crops like coffee, cotton, tea etc. meant that the peasant producers were now required to divide their time of agricultural production into cash and 'subsistence' crops.[6] Thus the shortage of food crops became a common feature culminating into permanent and semi-permanent famine conditions.[7] In Tanzania, for instance, its own agricultural production no longer meets the national demands, forcing the government to import foodstuffs in order to offset the domestic deficit.[8] Nevertheless, the shortage of foreign exchange limits the amount of imported foodstuffs, which is due to the fluctuation of world market prices for the main export crops.[9]

Besides the export crops like coffee, cotton, tea etc. produced by the peasants, others like sisal were introduced as plantation crops.[10] One essental characteristic of the plantation system is that production requires a sizeable resident labour force.[11] Juxtaposed to the traditional economy in Tanzania, where a proletarian class did not exist, the institution of plantation system required the creation of conditions for the emergence of free labour that was separated from the means of production. However, the creation of a sizeable labour force did not emerge. The European plantation owners expected the peasants to flock to their plantations through normal market mechanisms.[12]
But to their surprise, the market mechanisms did not

resolve the paradox of "actual shortage in the presence of the deceptive appearance of plenty."[13]

During my teaching days at Korogwe from 1976 to 1977 there were recruiting campaigns by the Tanzania Sisal Authority (TSA) in the Tanga region and the country at large for labourers in its sisal plantations. This was the time of the world market boom for sisal and the TSA was trying to bring all its plantations into full production.[14] In the Daily News Paper[15] of 17th April 1978, the TSA required about 5,000 workers to meet the immediate requirements of its 64 estates. The TSA managed to get only 3,000 workers. After two months it was reported that only 10 % of those obtained were still working. The rest of the workers had run away.[16]

The colonial pattern of economic exploitation also perpetuated social inequalities and imbalances among the different regions of the country and within the different parts of a region itself. Socio-economic facilities such as schools, hospitals, transport, agricultural extension services etc. were concentrated in those areas of colonial economic interests.[17] Walter Rodney points out that the map 'Inside Tanganyika' showing the major cotton and coffee growing areas in the country, virtually coincided with a map showing the areas in which colonial education was available.[18]

Concomitant with the changes in the economic base, came changes in the social structure. The economic system could not function without a corresponding political and ideological mechanism to justify the exploitative relations of production. This was the function of the colonial state apparatus, including the education system.[19]

The foundations of the present-day system of education in Tanzania were laid by the activities of Christian missionaries towards the end of the last century. The missionaries were interested in propagating Christianity and training African priests and considered themselves involved in a 'civilising mission'.[20] It was through these activities that missionary education first facilitated the separation of the African from his traditional society for the absorption into the colonial socio-economic system.

The growth of the colonial political and administrative apparatus also contributed significantly to the social differentiation of the indigenous people. The expansion of the state apparatus resulted in an expanding demand for local personnel. The only qualification required to become a clerk or a teacher was adequate education. Thus education became a major instrument in the formation of the petty bourgeoisie in Tanzania.[21]
Colonial education imbued its recipients with foreign culture, and inculcated them with bourgeois individualism and worship of the cash-nexus. However it also offered some of them the opportunity to come into contact with liberal and progressive ideas; with notions of bourgeois democracy, freedom and even socialism.[22]

Although the colonial education put the educated African elite in a somewhat better economic position than the rest of the population, the colonial system was incapable of satisfying the aspirations of this group.[23] It is not surprising that it was this same group of educated Africans which led the struggle against the colonial system.

The trend of the relationship between the people in the rural areas and the nationalist leaders who took

over political power from colonialism is also significant
to examine in order to understand the limitations facing
the government in its efforts to bring about rural development.
For instance, since the attainment of political independence in 1961, Tanzania's development efforts have been directed towards the rural areas where the majority of the population live. 88 % of the population of the country live in the rural areas and 83 % of them depend on agricultural activities for their livelihood.[24] But recent studies[25] on the early post-independence rural government policies show that these policies were characterised as failures, usually attributed to inadequate administration and planning.
Furthermore, from the Arusha Declaration in 1967 up to about 1973, the emphasis of the country's rural development policies was towards the creation of 'Ujamaa' villages. These were intended to be a particular type of rural communities with the intention of fostering as much as possible aspects of joint communal production by the villages and gradually reducing the share of production resulting from individual smallholders.

Nevertheless, according to the 'Villages and Ujamaa Villages Act' of 1975, one or another form of Block farming[26] is now considered sufficient for a village to become officially identified as an 'Ujamaa' village. This modification of policy has been taken by some recent studies[27] on 'Ujamaa' development in both the Tanga region and Tanzania at large as a failure of the policy to bring about rural socialism. It is argued that the concept of 'Ujamaa', which was intended to convey a social ideal of collective ownership of the means of production, has been reduced to a state of affairs in which individual farming is intermittently supplemented

by occasional cooperation in such tasks as planting and harvesting.[28]
The Party and government on the other hand do not admit to this failure.[29] The modification of policy was made to cope up with the existing economic crisis facing the country, whose causes are said to be beyond the control of the people of Tanzania. These uncontrollable causes include: bad weather conditions, high import oil prices and fluctuations in world market prices for the country's main export crops.[30]

1.1. Aims of the Study

An insight into the above-posed areas of investigation is likely to be gained satisfactorily through a case study of the historical experiences of one region in Tanzania where colonial economic exploitation began.[31] This work will attempt to analyse the socio-economic developments discussed in the past section with respect to the Tanga region. The purpose is to examine the reaction of the people in the rural areas of the region to development processes provoked by external factors including the government (both colonial and post-colonial). The findings of the issues investigated at regional and national level will later be related to existing general theories on the question of rural development in Africa.

Besides drawing illustrations from different parts of the region, the study aims at making a comparison between two districts of the region with different production systems: one producing mainly 'subsistance' crops (Handeni District) and the other (Korogwe District) with a large concentration of export crops.

The tribal character of the two districts is also interesting for a sociological study. Korogwe has a heterogenous tribal character, while one tribe is dominant in Handeni, i.e. the Wazigua people.
Moreover, the study proceeds with a realisation that rural development cannot be fully achieved without an analysis of the problems of industrialization, especially the importance of an internal production of a technology for the rural areas which is not too expensive and not too advanced in relation to the resource base of the rural masses. However, the problems of industrialization in the region lie outside the scope of this work. The focus is on the peasant farmers who are the main agricultural producers and who ultimately determine the volume produced and the quantity sold on the official market.

1.2. Hypotheses

The study is based on the following hypotheses:
(i) There is an argument[32] that the rural areas of Tanzania are characterised by a surplus of labour power which is underemployed. Hence it would be advisable to engage the underemployed people in productive economic activities such as wage labour in sisal plantations which require a lot of labour power.
This hypothesis is based on lack of information concerning the working conditions in the sisal plantations. I would like to argue in this work that very few peasants from the local tribes of the Tanga region, where most of the sisal plantations in the country are located, prefer to work in them. This is because the plantations do not offer them

any social security, the wages are low and the working conditions are very poor.

(ii) Another hypothesis frequently advanced is that the state in Tanzania has always responded to popular needs of the masses in the rural areas with the objective of increasing agricultural production.[33] I would also like to argue that it is the rural masses who are forced to respond to the needs of the state. This response has always been characterized by apathy. In the Tanga region this is shown by the peasants' resistance to export-crop production and communal 'development' activities.

1.3. Motivation to undertake the study

My life in the Tanga region, first as a child and later as a Tutor at the Korogwe College of National Education contributed greatly to my desire to undertake this study. My home village, Mkomazi, is about 20 km from the sisal estates at Mkumbara and Mazinde. I was always amazed by the dominance of workers from outside the region in these estates. When the sisal industry began to decline in the mid 1960s because of the world market problems, a number of these workers began to settle in the neighbouring villages as peasant farmers or as wage labourers in the rice farms of the local people.

In addition, before 1964 every male adult in Tanzania above eighteen years of age had to pay direct tax. It was common for us in the villages to see our parents and other elder relatives hide themselves in order to avoid the tax collectors. The latter were often accompanied by policemen.
The villagers were also under the pressure of agricul-

tural extension officers who moved from house to house forcing people to go and tend their cotton fields. In mid 1970s the villagers also had to be forced to move to new village areas selected by the government authorities.

These observations led me to develop an interest to investigate the causes of the above trends and if possible offer some tentative suggestions.

1.5. Organisation of the Study

The study is organised in the following parts:
The first part (Chapter II) makes a critical analysis of the different theoretical approaches to the questions of wage-labor and rural development in Tanzania and Africa at large. It also presents the methods used to collect empirical data for the study.
Chapter III gives a general overview of the general characteristics of the region, i.e. location, size, physiography, climate, population structure and the social organisations of the local people. This overview of the region is important because it helps the reader to comprehend the nature of the areas under-study and some of the aspects to be analysed in the rest of the work.
Chapter IV examines the response of the local peasants to wage-labour in the sisal plantations. It starts with a discussion of the different theories concerning wage-labour in Africa. It then looks at the introduction of the sisal industry in the region and background to the wage-labour question in the plantations; the nationalization policy (1967) and the characteristics of wage-labour in the present sisal plantation system in Tanzania;

theories on African working class struggles and workers' struggles in the plantations.

Chapter V investigates the historical development of the relationship between the government and the peasants especially the reaction of the latter to the different government programmes on rural development. The aspects to be investigated are: theories on the African peasantry and their application to the Tanzanian experience especially in the Tanga region. The latter includes background to peasant-export production; the post-independence peasant agricultural production; the improvement and transformation approach, Ujamaa and cooperative movements; and distribution of agricultural extension services, health, education and water facilities.

Chapter VI presents the general conclusions to the study and tentative suggestions.

Footnotes for Chapter One

1. Gwendolen M. Carter, 'African Studies in the United States 1955-1975', Vol. VI, pp. 2-5; Thomas Hodgkin, 'Where the Paths Began', in C. Fyfe (ed.), African Studies since 1945: A Tribute to Basil Davidson, Longman Group, London 1976, pp. 22 22-25.

2. David Goddard, 'Limits of British Anthropology', New Left Review, 58, November-December 1969, pp. 79-89.

3. As a result of the rising prices for staple food crops and nutritional problems in at least 22 African countries, the classical subsistence crops like cereals are not only marketed but are also exported.

4. Ruvuma, Kigoma and Mtwara regions were labour reserves for the sisal plantations in the Tanga region.

5. Michaela von Freyhold, 'Ujamaa Villages in Tanzania, An Analysis of a Social Experiment', Heinemann, London 1979, p. 15.

6. T. Szentes, The Political Economy of Underdevelopment, Budapest, Third Edition, 1976, p. 21.

7. B. D. Bowles, Export Crops and Underdevelopment in Tanganyika, in Utafiti, Journal of Faculty of Arts and Social Sciences, U.D.S.M., Vol. 1, No. 1, 1976, p. 8.

8. GTZ, Lower Mkomazi Irrigation Project, Main Report, Eschborn, FRG, January 1982, p. 20.

9. Wolfgang Schneider-Barthold, 'Farmers' Reactions to the Present Economic Situation in Tanzania: A Case Study of Villages in the Kilimanjaro Region, GDI, Berlin, Juni 1983, p. 1.

10. J. Rweyemamu, 'Underdevelopment and Industrialization in Tanzania, A Study of Perverse Capitalist Industrial Development, Exford University Press, London 1973, p. 16.

11. Ibid, p. 17.

12. Ibid, p. 17.

13. W. A. Lewis, 'Economic Development with Unlimited Supply of Labour, The Manchester School 1956, p. 14.

14. Hassan O. Kaya, 'Effectiveness of the existing Sisal-based Industries in Reducing the Market Dependence of the Sisal Industry in Tanzania: A Case Study of the Tanga Region Industries, M. A. Thesis, U.D.S.M. (Unpublished), 1978, p. 53.

15. Daily News, 17th April, 1978, p. 1. Daily News is the official Government News Paper in Tanzania.

16. Daily News, 13th June, 1978, p. 1.

17. T. Szentes, op. cit., p. 17.

18. W. Rodney, How Europe Underdeveloped Africa, T.P.H., Dar es salaam 1972, p. 266

19. For an analysis of the class structure under colonialism in Tanzania, see Issa G. Shivji, Tanzania: The Class Struggle Continues (Mimeo), Dar es salaam 1973, pp. 32-54.

20. K. F. Hirji, School Education and Underdevelopment in Tanzania, in Maji Maji, No. 12, Sept. 1973, p. 3.

21. Ibid, p. 5.

22. The early leadership of TAA and TANU the nationalist movements in Tanganyika were mostly composed of educated Africans. See J. Illife, Tanzania under German and British Rule, in Cliffe and Saul (ed), Socialism in Tanzania, EAPH, 1972, Vol. I, p. 14.

23. K. F. Hirji, op. cit., p. 5.

24. GTZ, 'Lower Mkomazi Irrigation Project, Main Report, Escborn, FRG, January 1982, p. 20.

25. G. Ibbott, 'Rural Development Programmes in Tanzania: The Case of Ruvuma Region, (Mimeo), DSM, pp. 3-7; H. Newiger, 'Evaluation of the Villagization Policies in Tanzania, (Mimeo), DSM, 1968; R. Dumont, 'Tanzania Agriculture After the Arusha Declaration, National Institute of Agronomy, Paris 1970, pp. 7-13.

26. Block farming is the term used when a sizeable area is cultivated for particular common crops but each family maintains responsibility for the cultivation and proceeds of its block.

27. F. M. Lofchie, 'Agrarian Crisis and Economic Liberalisation in Tanzania, in Journal of Modern African Studies, 11, 3(1978), pp. 451-75; Andrew Coulson (ed.), 'African Socialism in Practice - The Tanzania Experience, Heinemann 1979.

28. John Connel, 'The Evolution of Tanzanian Rural Development, ERB, UDSM, 1976, p. 4.

29. J. K. Nyerere, Ten Years After Arusha, DSM, pp. 6-7.

30. President Nyerere's Speech in Mwanza on Food Crisis, on 26/3/1981.

31. H. O. Kaya, op. cit., pp. 18-22.

32. C. W. Guilleband, 'An Economic Survey of the Sisal Industry of Tanzania, TSGA, England 1966; E. F. Hitchcock, Notes on the Sisal Industry, Tanga, No. 2, 1967.

33. I. M. Kaduma, Twenty Years of TANU Education, in G. Ruhumbika (ed.), Towards Ujamaa, Twenty Years of TANU Leadership, EALB, 1974, pp. 219-220.

II. THEORETICAL APPROACHES AND METHODOLOGY OF THE STUDY

2.1. Theoretical Approaches

There are two common approaches applied in the study of socio-economic development in Africa: one is based on an analysis of social classes in the society examined (this will be shown later in this section by the works of H. Bernstein, C. Ake etc.); and the other approach does not use the concept of social classes but looks social development in terms of social status groups, income groups and target groups (see for example studies on rural development in Africa by the World Bank).

V. I. Lenin gave the following integrated definition of social classes:

> "Classes are large groups of people differing from each other by the place they occupy in the historically determined system of social production, by their relations (in most cases fixed and formulated in law) to the means of production, by their role in the social organization of labour, and consequently by the dimensions of the share of social wealth which they dispose and the mode of acquiring it ... Classes are groups of people one of which can appropriate the labour of another owing to the different places they occupy in a definite system of social economy." 1

According to this definition social classes are characterised by the following distinctive economic and social features:

(i) they are groups of people that are distinguished primarily by their place in the historically determined system of social production. This means that every social class must be regarded in connection with the mode of production by which it is engendered, and that each system of production creates its own specific division of society into social classes (slave owners and slaves, feudal lords and serfs, capitalists and proletarians).

(ii) the relationship of the social classes to the means of production also depends on their role in the social organisation of labour.

For example, the capitalist system of social production is divided into two dominant social groups, i.e. one group which owns or controls the available means of production in society, and the other which essentially has no means of production except labour power. We shall not go into how the distribution of the means of production gets to be so unevenly distributed, instead we shall look at the major implications of this uneven distribution of the means of production.

Those who have only labour power and have no other means of production must produce to survive. This can only be done by selling their labour power to those who own or control the means of production in exchange for a wage. The latter buy the labour power in so far as they pay the wage earners less than what their labour power produces. This is the basis of exploitation in the capitalist system of production. The class which owns or controls the means of production is the bourgeoisie and those who sell their labour power are the proletarians.

In our application of the concept of social classes to Africa, we shall start with the characteristics of the dominant class, i.e. the bourgeoisie: Its most important general characteristics have to be analysed within the context of the peculiarities of the capitalism of the African economies, especially their dependent status in relation to the global capitalist system.[2] Capitalism in Africa could be described as derivative. It is deri-

vative in the sense that it developed as an effect
of the quest by the western European capitalists for
markets, raw materials and profits. It is capitalism
grafted on to a society in which the development of
the forces of production were still very rudimentary.
It is also derivative in the sense that much of the
capital, the technology and even the entrepreneural
skills come from abroad. This is because during colonialism the economy was not developed, but was merely
exploited. Moreover, the access of the indigenous people
to the control of production was strictly limited. Consequently, the indigenous bourgeoisie was very small
and weak.[3]

Various analysts have classified the indigenous bourgeoisie in Africa in different ways: One important tendency
has been to emphasize the subordination of this class
to the international bourgeoisie, referring to it as
a comprador class, i.e. it serves the interests of international capital and can only survive in this inferior
role.[4]

A contrary perspective has been to see the indigenous
bourgeoisie as a prospective 'national bourgeoisie'
struggling to free itself from foreign control and develop
the productive forces of its own society. Although this
role has been seen in the context of the third world
as a whole, some scholars have been hesitant about its
application to Africa. One of these scholars is Issa
Shivji, who says:
> "The so-called 'national bourgeoisie' in Africa ...
> are neither national nor bourgeois. They lack both
> the historical maturity of their metropolitan counter-
> part and the latter's objective economic base. The
> natural process of the development of the authentic
> national bourgeoisie and the national capitalism
> in Africa was irreversibly arrested by these countries
> coming into contact with advanced capitalism." [5]

It is further argued that most of the African states are too small, have too narrow resource bases, lack adequate capital and technical expertise, and have no tradition of capitalist behaviour to develop a national bourgeoisie.[6]

However, another concept found in recent literature to describe the indigenous bourgeoisie in Africa is that of 'bureaucratic bourgeoisie'.[7] The proponents of this concept contend that, because of the weaknesses of the indigenous bourgeoisie discussed above, they are unable to follow the classic pattern of development through private ownership of capital. Instead, a new path is followed in which the state becomes the mechanism through which the bourgeoisie controls capital and labour and by means of which it appropriates and accumulates surplus, i.e. it has been able to flourish only through a close attachment to the state.

Another concept which is commonly used to describe the dominant class in Africa is that of petty bourgeoisie. In the Communist Manifesto, Marx and Engels lumped a variety of different categories into this class, i.e. from petty producers such as shoemakers and owners of petty capital like shopkeepers, to the servants of capital who do not possess any capital themselves (professionals, managers, administrators, army officers etc.). They characterised them as an unstable class, in the process of polarisation with most of its members being plunged down into the ranks of the proletariat.[8] In contemporary Africa, the petty bourgeoisie has often been seen as the strongest indigenous class, and as the class that provides the leadership for nationalist movements, inheriting political power at the time of decolonisation. Nevertheless, it is generally agreed that its main interest is to transform itself into a bourgeoisie proper. Although some scholars contend that the results of its efforts have been varied. It has failed in Ghana[9] and succeeded in Nigeria.[10] In Tanzania it has succeeded to become a bureaucratic bourgeoisie.[11]

Moreover, attention has also been paid to the internal fractions of the African petty bourgeoisie: a commercial class of small traders, shopkeepers, lorry and tax owners etc.; a rural petty bourgeoisie defined similar to the kulak peasant class; and a bureaucratic petty bourgeoisie of civil servants, teachers etc. Some scholars like Amilcar Cabral held out the possibility that the petty bourgeoisie in Africa may orient itself downwards rather than upwards, linking its interests to those of peasants and workers in opposition to the international bourgeoisie.[12]
This idea of the possibility of the African petty bourgeoisie 'committing class suicide' originated from the influence of Maoist theory, although the proponents of this idea in Africa often neglect the subordinate role Mao himself designated to the revolutionary petty bourgoisie in his 3-class alliance theory of revolutionary forces.[13] Furthermore, the idea of petty bourgeois 'Class suicide' in Africa has mostly been propagated by African petty bourgeois intellectuals with a stronger commitment to Marxism as a vision of social change rather than as a tool of social analysis. This is shown by their emphasis on proletarian ideology rather than to the proletarian class, as the key to revolutionary success.[14]

Before concluding our discussion of the dominant social classes in Africa, it is also reasonable to mention those surving holders of traditional authority who continue to be significant in different parts of Africa. While their political power may have been lost (as in the case of Tanzania) their ideological power still

remains because their former subjects change their attitudes gradually. Moreover, those who were able to use their traditional influence successfully have joined the bourgeoisie and those with less luck found themselves pushed into salaried office-holding or joined the ranks of the oppressed.[15] Having examined the dominant classes in Africa, we can now turn to the oppressed:
The orthodox Marxist theorists maintain that in many countries of Africa, the small producers have lost their rights in rural land through land alienation or overpopulation, and that there are several generations of families which have grown up and worked in the urban areas. Therefore, the African urban work force is much more stable and committed to paid employment than is commonly supposed.[16]

Their opponents on the other hand, argue that workers in Africa do not constitute a permanent, urbanized, proletarianized class, but an amorphous collection of migrant workers with rights to land in rural areas, hence not fully separated from their means of production. In short their argument is that true proletarians with only their labour to exchange for a wage are only just emerging in Africa.
They go on to argue that far from being exploited, the urban workers in Africa, are a highly paid 'labour aristocracy' attuned to political conservatism by being better off than the 'wretched of the earth' in the rural areas.[17] Eliot Berg gives the following general benefits of urban life for the workers:
> "... however low their income and welfare by some absolute yardstick African wage earners are in general a relatively privileged group in African society. They enjoy more of the benefits of modernisation and growth than any other African social group. They have available and better medical care, a larger share of the conveniences and amusements of modern life - from supermarkets to cinemas." 18

Several social scientists who have made studies on the urban rural income differences in Africa and other developing countries do not accept the above thesis of 'labour aristocracy'. Egbert Gerken points out two unique characteristics sited in the literature on the problem of employment in developing countries. These are chronic and open unemployment especially in towns and extreme income differences between unskilled labourers employed in 'organised sectors' and those in 'informal sectors'. He defines the 'informal sectors' of employment as follows:
>"Hier sollen zum informalen Sektor sämtliche Betriebe am urbanen Standort gezählt werden, die überwiegend Familienarbeitskräfte beschäftigen und deren Lohnarbeitskräfte nicht durch gesetzliche oder tarifliche Regelungen des Lohnsatzes und der übrigen Arbeitsbedingungen geschützt werden." 19

The labour aristocracy thesis has been used to cast doubt on the efficacy of the working class in Africa as a revolutionary class. It is based on a comparison of rural and urban incomes as evidence of class differences. It does not take into consideration that the real living standards of the urban workers in Africa are not on the average significantly higher than those of the rural masses. Higher costs of living in the present urban areas of Africa, transfer of income from urban workers to rural families, and the greater insecurity of the worker compared to the peasant, have all been ignored by the propagators of the 'labour aristocracy' theory.[20]

Peter Waterman gives the same conclusion that the economically privileged position of the African workers has been exaggerated and that the political consciousness and activities of this class have been more radical than is often claimed.[21]

Giovanni Arrighi and John Saul examined the concept
of 'semi-proletarianised peasant' in Africa. They divided the working class in Africa into two distinctive
groups:
(i) the 'proletariat proper' are seen generally as
a small minority who receive incomes sufficiently
high to justify a total break of their links with
the peasantry.
(ii) the 'semi-proletarianised' peasantry as wage earners
who are only marginally or partially proletarianised
over their life, and they derive the bulk of their
means of subsistence for their families from outside
the wage economy. They point out that in the socialist debate and research, attention has been focused
on the proleariat proper. The semi-proletarianised
peasantry was largely forgotten.[22]

In his contribution to the discussion on workers' participation in management in Tanzania, Pius Msekwa pointed
out that the slow development of workers' participation
in management in Tanzania was partly due to the fact
that the country achieved her independence with one
of the least formally educated populations in Africa,
a very small industrial sector, and an exclusive Asian
community in control of what local business there was.
The question of the effective participation of the workers in the management of the organisations in which
they were employed came with to the fore only after
the Arusha Declaration which placed the major means
of production under public control.[23]

Nonetheless, little was done in this direction for about
three years after the Arusha Declaration for the following
reasons given by Arnold Temu:
> "the country was too preoccupied with the mechanics
> of taking up or setting up and expanding the enter-

prises nationalised. Secondly, ... the attitudes
and methods of those who were appointed to run these
institutions, even though they were Tanzanians, continued to be the same as those of the colonial manager;
and their relationship with the worker was the same
as that of the colonial manager." 24

P. L. Lawrence showed how the workers in various work
places in Tanzania aided by Clause 15 of the Party Guidelines on workers' participation in management,[25] went
beyond wage demands and directed their strikes against
unsystematic management, lack of consultation, and comman-
dism of the work place.[26]

In their analysis of rural differentiation in Africa,
John Saul and Rogger Woods define peasants as those
who have some family rights to control of the means
of production, and who also use these means of production
to produce some output for the market. This definition
enables them to differentiate peasants from other social
classes in the rural areas: (i) the rural proletariat,
who have been wholly separated from the means of production
and can only sell their labour power; (ii) subsistence
farmers and (iii) rural capitalists who buy and sell
means of production.
They also relate these rural social groups to varying
political interests and activities. They emphasize the
need for detailed case studies to the problems of the
rural social classes in order to examine the actual
political potential of the different groups in different
production areas.[27]

Henry Bernstein also argues that the varieties of the
peasantry, of local conditions and of political and
economic interests call for a variety of rural development strategies. This is needed because these differences
indicate the heterogeneity of the conditions and forms

of peasant production, the dangers of generalizing them,
and the necessity of investigating particular peasantries
to examine their relations with other forms of production,
the state and their place in the overall development
of commodity relations.[28]

Uma Lele made a comparative evaluation of 17 sets of
rural development projects and programmes in Sub-Saharan
Africa, including Tanzania, involving the participation
of a number of multilaterial, bilateral and national
agencies. She defines rural development as:
> "the improvement of the living standards of the mass
> of the low-income population residing in rural areas
> and making the process of their development self-
> sustaining." [29]

The above definition has the following implications:
(i) improvement of the living standards of the subsistence
population involves mobilization and allocation of resources so as to reach a desirable balance over time
between the welfare and productive services available
to the subsistence of the rural sector; (ii) mass participation requires that resources be allocated to low-income
areas and social classes and that productive and social
services actually reach them; (iii) making the process
of self-sustaining requires development of the appropriate
skills and implementing capacity and the presence of
institutions at the local, regional and national levels
to ensure effective use of existing sources and to forster
the mobilization of additional financial and human resources for continued development of the subsistence
sector. Self-sustenance thus means involving, as distinct
from simply reaching, the subsistence populations through
development programmes.

The first investments in the development of the low

income subsistence agriculture in Africa were prompted
by the objective of increasing production of export
crops in the smallholder sector. They were financed
by European commercial companies, development corporations
or the governments of former colonial countries. In
these export-crops schemes, the agricultural services
of extension, credit, inputs, marketing, and processing
were administered through project authorities or parastatal
organisations. Examples of these programms are the Kenya
Tea Development Programme and the development of smallholder tobacco production in Urambo and Tungi in Tanzania.

Uma Lele further classified the regional rural development programmes into two types: (i) integrated rural
development undertaken mainly on the initiative of donor
agencies and planned and administered by expatriates;
(ii) regional development programmes undertaken with
substantial initiative and participation of the national
governments.[30]
The application of the strategy of integrated rural
development to Africa was elaborated in a United Nations
publication (Integrated Approach to Rural Development
in Africa - E/CN.14/SWSA/8) and further elaborated in
detail at the African Regional Conference on the Integrated
Approach to Rural Development, held at Moshi in Tanzania
in October 1969.

As the phrase 'integrated rural development' suggests,
it involves the focusing of development efforts on the
transformation of rural society. This is justified by
the fact that more than 70 % of Africa's population
live in the rural areas, and that agriculture is the
mainstay of Africa's economy. It is assumed that the
focusing of development on rural society is necessary
to ensure that the maximum benefit to the masses as

well as the growth of the entire economy.

The word integrated implies that all aspects of development are co-ordinated and flow together to form an unbroken whole. This type of development is analogous to an assembly line production, where all the parts and sub-assemblies must arrive at the right place at the right time if production of the finished product is to be facilitated. The need for an integrated approach to rural development is said to be necessary given the conditions of rural societies in Africa which do not favour conventional planning methods. For instance, the rural population in Africa is dispersed over a wide area in isolated pockets. These dispersed populations have to be integrated to some extent so that certain minimal infrastructure necessary for promoting development can be viable. This is because to increase productivity in the rural areas, it is necessary to upgrade health services, improve tools and techniques of production, combat some superstitious attitudes etc. In short, the process of rural development and the magnitude of the problem of promoting economic and social progress in the rural areas requires that inter-related programmes for the promotion of agriculture, education and training, health and nutrition, community development etc. must be planned and executed in a co-ordinated fashion taking into account of the effect that development programmes in one area are likely to have on other areas.[31]

However, the concept of rural integrated development has faced different operational definitions in different African countries.
Claude Ake gives an example of the manifesto of one of the leading political parties in the Nigerian election of 1979 which had a proposal for integrated rural develop-

ment, whose purpose was the capitalisation of agriculture. In several African countries all sorts of projects of rural development are called integrated rural development, although they are widely different.[32] It is perhaps the vagueness of the concept and its suggestion of a progressive stance which accounts for its popularity among African policy makers. It is clearly progressive to focus development in the rural areas where most of the population lives and where the most elementary necessities are lacking, but the idea is trivialised by the types of programmes designated as integrated rural development schemes. The idea has become an ideology which confers legitimacy to existing political systems by acknowledging the need for change while promoting only marginal changes.[33]

The Tanga Regional Development Plan (1975-1980) makes a comprehensive examination of the socio-economic development of the Tanga Region within the same context of integrated rural development. Tanzania was supposed to be one of the few countries in Africa to have taken the idea of integrated rural development fairly seriously by having made efforts to give attention to the development of its rural areas, and introduce into the countryside changes which if successful would have meant a significant improvement in the welfare of the rural people in Tanzania. These changes were not made in the name of integrated rural development but with the aim of promoting socialism and self-reliance.

The steps taken to implement this idea included the consolidation of the rural populations into bigger villages called 'Ujamaa villages'. But the results of the villagization policy have been rather ambiguous. The consolidation of the rural population into the new villages was often hastily and crudely done by overzealous officials, with the result that it caused apathy on the part of the rural people. In their analysis of the Tanzania's policy of rural socialism Henry Mapolu and Phillipson showed how class contradictions marred the policy's good intentions. They show an unfortunate trend away from the participation and initiative at grass-roots level and the ever greater concentration of power in the hands of the bureaucracy, despite that the official policy puts considerable emphasis on peasant initiatives in the formation and management of the 'Ujamaa villages'.[34]

Rosemary Galli points out that studies in Columbia, Mexico and Papaloapan have shown that the strategy of integrated rural development is meant to manipulate the peasants psychologically in order to put them passively on land, where possible make them more productive. According to her this strategy came as a result of the recognition by the governments and international agencies that subsidies and aid to rural entrepreneurs did not automatically lead to savings, faster accumulation or growth. Thus the governments of Tanzania, Columbia and Mexico with the support of the World Bank and other international agencies have turned to developing a 'middle peasantry' through enforcing savings on these peasants through credit and market structures.[35]

A study on 'Ujamaa in Tanzania' by Bruno Musti de Gennaro complements the studies on Columbia and Mexico. It shows the growth of state management in the rural areas and stresses the necessity of class analysis in understanding the struggle between the state and the peasants for control over agricultural product.[36] Henry Bernstein sees the different rural development schemes in Tanzania as:

"... a strategy of quasi-dispossession of the producers and the conversion of land and other means of production into state property." 37

In his discussion of the relationship between the state and the peasantry in Africa, Goran Hyden argues that the history of modernisation has been largely that of how to capture the peasants. According to his thesis, Africa is the only continent where the peasants have not yet been captured by other social classes. By being owners of their own means of production, the smallholder peasants in Africa have enjoyed a degree of independence from other social classes.[38]
This argument is doubtful because it fails to realise the fact that in most African countries one finds large numbers of peasants and small commodity producers who are not wage labourers and who may be said to own their means of production, but this ownership is only nominal, because they are easily compelled to submit to exploitation. A lot of people who exploit the peasants in the African economies do not themselves own the means of production, unless state power can be called a means of production. They are able to exploit because of their control of state power. The latter is used to control the means of production and to carry out exploitation. State power is used to regulate the conditions of peasant production by: (i) making laws about who might produce what; (ii) imposing agricultural development programmes which put the peasant in the position of using inputs such as fertilizer, and different techniques and tools. The process of compelling the peasants the use of these inputs and techniques aid the integration of the peasant into exploitative commodity relations; (iii) subordination and expropriating the peasant through mechanisms of exchange. These include crop grading, which determines the price, and those who control the grading system

are able to use it as a means of appropriation of peasant
surplus product. They can easily ensure that the peasant
producer gets much less than the value of his product.
The common form of subordination and expropriation of
the peasant producer is through monopolistic marketing
authorities of peasant crops. For instance, in Tanzania
each peasant crop has been put under a particular market
authority. These include Tea Authority, Coffee Authority,
Cashewnuts Authority, Cotton Authority, etc.

The official justification of these marketing organisations
is that the arrangement avoid price fluctuations during
the buying season because the minimum price payable
is announced ahead of the buying season and adhered
to it. This is expected to help stabilize the income
of the peasant producer and also helps to rationalise
his activities. Moreover, it is claimed that the regulation of the quality of commodities by these marketing
authorities, and the payment of higher prices for better
quality products, gives the producer incentives to produce
better quality products and to increase his earning
power. In reality the state through these marketing
authorities buys the peasant's products cheaply and
sells them to the foreign importers at much higher prices
and retains the difference to dispose of, as it sees
fit instead of passing it on to the peasant producer.
In this case, the peasants are self-employed but are
nevertheless compelled to submit to exploitation.

On the question of factors affecting labour flow into
smallholder agriculture in Africa, D. W. Norman says
that compared to Asia, labour availability in Africa
is frequently a greater constraint to increasing agricultural productivity than is the availability of land.[39]
This is supportes by John H. Cleaves who shows that

on an average, African smallholders devoted only about
1,000 man hours per adult per year to agricultural activities, compared to up to 3,000 man hours in several
Asian countries. He says that Africa is characterised
by a paradox of farm labour shortage and an apparent labour
surplus. This lies in the way the labour time is allocated, i.e. (a) the seasonality of labour usage, (b)
the allotment of time between farm work, non-farm activities, and leisure; and (c) the division of labour
between the sexes.[40] As far as sexual division of labour
is concerned, a study made by the United Nations Economic
Commission for Africa observed that women provide 60
to 80 per cent of the agricultural labour used in different
parts of Africa.[41] H. Cleave also sites numerous examples
which suggest that, compared to men, African women often
work longer both in the farm and non-farm activities.[42]

However, as a result of the introduction of new technological innovations it is not uncommon to find men
and women performing the same tasks during periods of
intense labour requirements. As far as the marketing
of agricultural output is concerned, a study financed
by the International Development Association in East
Africa in 1975 found that, inadequate marketing
and transport facilities, fragmented markets, and unpredictable prices are some of the major bottlenecks to
rural development. J. W. Mellor adds that most of the
marketing organisations in Africa find it easier to
handle export crops than food crops. This is because
export crops are easier to procure; their areas of production are endowed with relatively good marketing
infrastructure of roads, storage, and processing facilities. Furthermore, most marketing organisations lack
the administrative capacity and manpower required to
purchase small, scattered supplies of food crops and

frequently not interested in distributing procured food supplies beyond the big towns.[43]

An alternative to the improvement of marketing of food crops in the rural areas is the establishment of cooperative societies. But evaluation of the cooperative promotion in Africa has shown that in most African countries the training of cooperative staff fails to cover the trading and speculative aspects of the marketing of food crops. Moreover, the graduate of cooperative societies is handicapped when he goes to the field because the training he had acquired is not job oriented. This lack of adequate practical training sometimes becomes a source of frustration to the trainees. Therefore if the food marketing cooperatives are to survive, they have to be able to compete with the private trading channels in their ability to speculate and to operate at low costs in the highly fragmented domestic food markets.[44]

This work on the problems of rural development in the Tanga region bases its investigations mainly on the social classes analysis approach. The approach is useful for this study because of its historical perspective, especially with respect to the examination of the historical development of the wage-labour question in the sisal plantations and the relationship between the government and the peasantry in the region. Its macro-sociological view of society also helps to draw conclusions to the whole country.

Besides consulting the relevant literature on the different theories concerning the questions of wage-labour and rural development in Africa and Tanzania in particular, empirical data was collected on the basis of the two main hypothesis of the study: the migratory character

of wage-labour in the sisal plantations and the negative
response of the local peasantry in the region to socio-
economic development programmes from outside their own
communities.

2.2. Methodology

The following methods were used for data collection:
(i)   examination of archival reports and statistics;
(ii) group and individual interviews;
(iii) participatory observations.

2.2.1. Examination of Secondary Data

This study takes a historical approach to the problems
of socio-economic development in the Tanga region, therefore historical data on the region was required like
the pre-colonial social organisations, introduction
of the sisal industry and peasant export-crop production,
etc.
This data was obtained from the "Weltwirtschaftsarchiv"
in Hamburg, the Tanzania National Archives in Dar es
salaam and examination of literature in different libraries in Berlin and Dar es salaam.

Another aspect of this study is that it concentrates
on the problems of rural development in the region.
This is because the majority of the people in the region
live in the rural areas and agriculture is their main
activity.
Data on the rural development activities in the region
like 'Ujamaa development', education, health, agricultural extension services etc. was obtained from the

Tanga Integrated Rural Development Programme (TIRDEP) offices in Tanga and GTZ at Eschborn. TIRDEP is one of the prominent projects within the frame of bilateral technical cooperation between Tanzania and the Federal Republic of Germany.

The information from TIRDEP offices was supplemented by other documents from the 'Regional and District Development Directors' offices in Tanga, Korogwe and Handeni. These offices are responsible for all development activities in the region and districts. In order to get comparative data with national statistics contact with the Central Bureau of Statistics in Dar es salaam was made.

2.2.2. Interviews

The interviews conducted were a combination of both group and individual. This was particularly the case in the sisal plantations. This was based on the pretests made in two plantations (Mazinde and Toronto Sisal Estates in Korogwe district). The managers advised that due to the labour shortage facing most of the plantations in the region and the country at large, it would be difficult to interview individual labourers at work. It was advisable to organise group interviews with the labourers and then arrange with individuals among them for intensive interviews after work. However, group interviews are helpful in the sense that one gets many useful ideas at the same time and saves the problem of going around looking for individual interviewees. One disadvantage experienced during the study and which is common with this type of interview is that some individuals influence the opinions of others.[45]

As regards the individual interviews in both the plantations and the villages, a 'Multi-purpose Questionnaire' was used. This consisted of questions on the following modules:
(i)   a household roster which obtains a list of the household members, their family interrelationships, education and other basic demographic characteristics;
(ii) migration and employment data;
(iii) household income/assets.

The significance of each of these modules for the study and the limitations of collecting the necessary data for them will be presented in the following sections. First of all, the criteria for the selection of the sample sisal plantations, villages, and interviewees will be examined:

2.2.2.1. Selection of Sample Sisal Plantations and Labourers

In cooperation with the district authorities at Korogwe and Handeni and given restricted financial resources and the existing transport problems in the region, 7 sisal plantations out of 15 in Korogwe district, and 2 out of 3 in Handeni were selected for the survey. The basis of selection was their ownership pattern.

The sisal plantations in Tanzania have three forms of ownership: wholly state-owned through the Tanzania Sisal Authority; joint ventures between the government and private investors; and wholly privately owned (mostly by foreign investors).
4 of the selected plantations were state owned (Toronto, Mwelya, Ngombezi in Korogwe district and Kwamgwe in Handeni); 2 were joint ventures between the government

and the Ralli Company (Mazinde and Kwalukonge in Korogwe
district); and 3 were wholly privately owned (Kwamndulu,
Kwamdolwa and Kwaragulu) (see Table 2.1).

Table 2.1: The Surveyed Sisal Plantations in the Korogwe
and Handeni Districts (1983)

Name of Plantation	Ownership	District	Total No. of Workers (a)	Workers Interviewed	Key Persons (b)
TORONTO	TSA	KOROGWE	91	10	2
MWELYA	TSA	KOROGWE	56	6	2
NGOMBEZI	TSA	KOROGWE	95	7	1
KWAMNDOLWA	CATHOLIC SISTERS	KOROGWE	51	6	1
MAZINDE	Govt. of Tanz.(50%) & Rally Comp.(50%)	KOROGWE	76	9	2
KWALUKONGE	- " -	KOROGWE	58	7	2
KWAMNDULU	AMBONI GROUP CO.	KOROGWE	62	6	1
KWARAGURU	- " -	HANDENI	47	6	1
KWAMGWE	TSA	HANDENI	46	6	1
TOTAL			582	63	13

(a) = Total number of workers are those registered in the master-rolls and work-cards
(b) = The Key-persons interviewed were either managers or agricultural extension officers of the surveyed sisal plantations
TSA = Tanzania Sisal Authority

Source: The Surveyed Sisal Plantations and the TSA-Head-Office, Tanga

The selection of the interviewees in the plantations
was based on a 'bewußte Auswahl', i.e. the intention
was to interview labourers who had worked in the plantations for at least three years. The purpose was to
get information on the development of the living and
working conditions of the workers in the present sisal
plantation system.
The interviews were based on open questions with respect
to housing, transport, health, food and education facilities, wage levels, employment security etc. The
information from the labourers was compared with that
obtained from the management interviewed. Given the
labour shortage in the plantations three interviewees
were randomly selected from the different work-sections
of the plantations shown in the Master-Rolls and Work-
cards.[46]
The common problems in the surveyed plantations were
that some of the randomly selected interviewees appeared
on the Master Rolls but they had stopped working in
the plantations a long time ago. There were always contradictions on the data concerning the total number
of workers in the plantation between the figures given
by the key persons interviewed and those registered
on the Master-rolls.

However, some of the randomly selected interviewees
were still working on the plantations but failed to
attend the interviews because of sickness or other personal problems at home. Some of the substitutes selected refused to attend the interviews. A total number
of 63 randomly selected workers were interviewed in
the nine sisal plantations surveyed. After interviewing
more than 50 persons no new information was obtained,
so those who were interviewed were taken as representative.
Moreover, 13 Key-persons (managers and agricultural

extension officers of the surveyed plantations) were interviewed.

2.2.2.2. Selection of Sample Villages and Households

Korogwe district had 115 registered villages and the figure for Handeni was 102. The average size of the villages in both districts was 250 to 300 households. Table 2.2 shows the surveyed villages and households in the two districts.

Table 2.2: The Surveyed Villages and Households in the Korogwe and Handeni Districts (1983)

Name of Division	District	Total Villages	Surveyed Villages	Total Households	Surv. Househ.	Key (a) Persons
Bungu	Korogwe	31	5	9203	53	4
Korogwe	"	25	6	10997	58	5
Mombo	"	37	6	11559	62	5
Chanika	Handeni	8	5	3482	55	4
Kwekivu	"	13	3	3240	34	3
Sindeni	"	11	5	3300	43	3
TOTAL		125	30	41781	305	24

(a) = The Key-persons included: Village Party Chairmen, Party Secretaries, Village Managers, Old men and other Village Dignitaries.

Source: Surveyed Villages and Offices of the District Development Directors in Korogwe and Handeni

The selection of the divisions and villages surveyed
was based on their differences in ecology, good transport
links and production systems. These differences were
taken for comparison purposes. Three administrative
divisions were selected from each of the two districts,
i.e. Korogwe and Handeni.

In Korogwe district: Bungu division which lies in the
Usambara Mountains was selected because it is the only
division in the district where different export crops
like coffee, tea and cardamon are grown; Korogwe division
has good links and includes the district headquarters;
Mombo is the driest division in the district. It lies
along the Tanga line rail-road.

In Handeni district the divisions surveyed were: Chanika,
where the district headquarters is situated; Kwekivu
is very remote from the headquarters but it is a very
fertile area and different agricultural crops such as
tobacco, maize, bananas, cassava and sorghum are grown;
Sindeni division lies along the main road to Korogwe.
It has good transport links but it is one of the driest
parts in the district. 17 registered villages in Korogwe
were examined and 173 respondents were interviewed.
The figures for Handeni were 13 villages and 132 interviewees. This was due to the poor transport links in
the remote areas of Handeni and the fact that peasants
were in the middle of the planting season. The randomly
selected interviewees were more cooperative in Korogwe
than in Handeni with respect to willingness to be interviewed.

The interviewees in the surveyed villages were obtained
in the following way: In Tanzania each registered village
is politically and administratively organised in a cell

system. A cell being a cluster of ten to fifteen houses with a cell leader being responsible for it. The political head of the village is the Party Chairman. The village has also a Village Secretary who is responsible for daily administrative affairs.

The unit of interviews in the village was the head of the household or his representative, who could provide information about other members of the household. The names of the cell-leaders were obtained from the Village Secretary and each cell-leader provided the names of the heads of households in his cell. A random sampling of 30 heads in each village was made. The arrangements to meet the randomly selected interviewees were made through the assistance of the Village Secretary and the cell leaders.

The following sections will examine in detail the limitations faced in collecting information for the main aspects investigated in the individual interviews, namely: household roster, migration and employment and income and assets of the household.

2.2.2.3. Identification of the household

Information about the size and characteristics of members of a household is significant for the analysis of the living conditions of the people, labour force, children of school age and sources of income for the household.

The first problem was to identify the particular household. This is because the nature of the household varies considerably across the regions of the country and within the different tribal groups of the same region.[47]
For instance, C. Clark defines the household as:
> "those persons who live together and eat together regularly." [48]

Whereas J. Neil restricts the concept of household to persons who share income and expenses.[49] Sometimes the household is taken to mean persons related by blood, marriage or adoption.[50]

The above definitions are very controversial because in some areas in Tanzania and Africa at large, there are family members who are related to each other and may have close economic ties without living under one roof or eating together.[51] Among the Wasukuma people of Tanzania, for example, husbands and wives may maintain separate 'miji' (dwellings) and/or separate finances. Moreover, in some of the villages surveyed along the Mkomazi River Valley (Korogwe district) like Mkomazi, Mkumbara and Mazinde, related families lived in the same compound but did not eat together or share income.

As a result of the contraversy of identifying a household, the criteria of identifying the household used in this study was based on the definition given by Deborah Freedman and Eva Müller who had faced the same problem in their study. They define the household as consisting of persons who live in close proximity, share a kitchen and food and at least a major part of income and expenses.[52] On the basis of this definition, the list of the members of the households surveyed in the study consisted of persons who usually resided in the household. Persons temporarily absent were included, while temporary guests found there at the date of interview were excluded.

One important aspect with respect to the data on household was that of age structure of the members. Age structure is significant for determination of children of school age and people able to work. However, the problem

faced was to obtain accurate age reports. This is because
of the low level of literacy in the rural areas. There
were cases in which the interviewee did not know his
or her own age let alone that of other members of the
household. The interviewees were encouraged as much
as possible to consult family records. For instance,
if the head of the household remembered when one member
of the household was born, he was also asked to remember
how old he/she was when that person was born.

2.2.2.4. Migration

As far as the question of migration in the rural areas
was concerned, the study was interested in two aspects:
the determinants and consequences of migration. The
data was meant to help make comparison between groups
with varying migration experiences, especially between
the indigenous people of the Tanga region and other
tribal groups from outside the region.
The determinants of migration are of interest to social
scientists since it is often the prospects of finding
a better income which might cause a person or family
to move.[53]

However, to study the determinants of migration ideally
one needs to obtain longitudinal data which measures
the economic characteristics of the household and its
members at a particular time, and then the household
could be re-interviewed to determine any subsequent
migration of individual family members or households
as a whole during the next years.[54] This approach was
not possible within the constraint of a one time research
like the present one. One other important factor in
human resource analysis is the general character

of the place in which the individual migrant resided
during her/his formative years. This could furnish some
useful information about the type of migration and also
its determinants.

The interviewee was also asked about the employment
situation prior to his recent migration. This was meant
to privide some idea of whether the recent move was
for economic reasons or for other reasons. The identi-
fication of the characteristics and work experience
of individuals who undertake temporary moves was of
interest to the study for knowing the economic position
of their families. He/she was asked about the adequacy
and dependendability of the major source of employment,
i.e. whether the household relied on its farm or business
for subsistence or supplemented the income by other
kinds of work especially wage labour in the sisal plantations.

2.2.2.5. Employment

Despite that work is a salient aspect of peoples' lives,
it is difficult for people in the rural areas of a developing country like Tanzania with irregular employment patterns to recall the work experience over an
entire year. Accuracy could be improved if the same
household could be interviewed several times during
the year. This was not possible in a one time research
survey like this.

Moreover, in many developing countries underutilization
of labour is a serious problem but difficult to measure.[55]
This brought the need for determining the extent to
which the interviewees' employment situation was subject

to seasonal or other variations and factors. During the interviews the respondent was asked to report all the different kinds of work he/she had done in the past year.[56] A distinction was made between self or family employment and employment by someone else. This distinction was done because of the fact that in most developing countries some people work on their own account as well as for someone else during the same year.[57] For example, there were people who owned small private farms but worked as hired labourers for rich peasants or in the sisal plantations.

Furthermore, working for self was understood by most interviewees but there was need to know how close a relative must be and/or how close the work relation had to be in order to be considered family. In case of doubt, the interviewee was let to decide for himself whether he viewed his employer as a member of the family or primarily as an employer.

2.2.2.6. Income/Assets

In addition to data on migration and employment, the study had the objective of getting data on the economic status of the household. Nevertheless, like in other developing countries data on income is very difficult to collect in the rural areas of Tanzania.[58] This is because the interviewees do not pay income taxes or do not add up their various household earnings over a year. They generally have no idea of the accounting concepts which underlie the economists' definition of income.
Therefore, to measure the household's economic position data on its holdings on selected assets such as land,

cattle, quality of housing and farm equipment and other durables could be collected via observation. Whereas obtaining data on financial asset holdings and debts was not easy. However, one general problem with the use of assets as an indicator of economic status is that it is difficult to combine information on holdings of many different kinds of assets into a single quantitative measure. This is partly because families hold assets in many forms including their own dwelling units, land, cattle etc.[59] Most interviewees were neither willing nor able to report monetary values of all such holdings. Therefore, a realistic approach was to concentrate on the ownership and indication of the approximate order of magnitude of the holdings.

The most important asset in the rural areas is land. The study was interested in all land owned by the interviewees, whether or not the household was farming it at the time of the survey. Land farmed on tenancy or share cropping basis, but owned by others was excluded.

2.2.2.7. Key Persons

Interviews were also conducted with persons in the district and regional offices responsible for education, health, agricultural extention services, marketing, 'Ujamaa Development'. Discussions were also made with Village Chairmen and Secretaries and old key persons in the surveyed village about the traditional social organisations of the area, different national development programmes like 'Ujamaa-Socialism', export/food crop production, marketing of agricultural crops, agricultural extension services, adult education campaigns etc.

One limitation of the interviews with the key persons mentioned above was to get the interviewees at the appointed time. There were cases in which interviews with some officers had to be done by telephone because the interviewee was not available in his office at the agreed time. The interviews in such cases were not detailed because of expenses, particularly when it involved phoning from a distant place.

2.3. Participatory Observation

In order to get some experience of the activities done by the labourers in the sisal plantations and the peasants in the villages arrangements were made with the respective authorities to participate in some of these activities. This involved working in the decortication section where the sisal leaves are being processed into fibre and in a sisal nursery. This was done at Toronto and Mazinde Sisal Estates for a total of ten days. There was also an opportunity to visit the camps where the permanent workers live and to observe their living conditions, especially the quality of housing. Most of the houses are the ones built during the colonial days.

In the villages, participation in village activities involved taking part in communal activities which include harvesting sorghum at Kikunde village, Kwekivu division, Handeni district and transplanting rice at Mkomazi village in Korogwe district. The purpose was to observe the organisation of labour in the communal farms.

During break-time there was a chance to discuss with some of the labourers in the plantations about the working and living conditions in the present sisal plantation

system, and with the villagers about the problems and
disadvantages of socialist development in the rural
areas, export and food crop production etc. The problem
with participatory observation is that the beginning
is always difficult. One feels new to the people and the
latter could feel sceptical to begin with. However,
one way is to inspire confidence to the people by making
them know that the study was supposed to be a learning
experience and not an expert evaluation of their activities.
Moreover, it was not possible to note the important
ideas and observations at once.

2.4. Summary

Chapter Two started with an examination of the different
approaches and theories on the questions of wage-labour
and rural development in Africa and Tanzania in particular.
The theories included those which look the two questions
on the basis of social classes and those which do not
use the concept of social classes but approach social
development in terms of status groups, target groups
etc. It was also stated that this work will take the
approach based on social class analysis of society.
This is due to its historical perspective which is relevant to the issues investigated in the study.

The methods used to obtain data for this study included
examination of secondary data in archives and libraries
in Germany and Tanzania; interviews (both group and
individual), with randomly selected wage-labourers and
villagers in selected sisal plantations and villages.
The selection of the plantations was based on their
ownership patterns and that of the villages was based
on their ecology, transport links and production systems.

Interviews were also conducted with Key-persons responsible for different socio-economic development activities in the plantations, villages, districts and the region at large.

The other method used to collect data was through participating in some of the activities done by the labourers in the plantations and peasants in the villages.

As a result of the low level of education in the rural areas it was difficult to get exact data on aspects like age structure, employment and income. Some of the interviewees did not attend the interviews for various reasons like sickness or refused to be interviewed, while others, especially the key persons were not available at the appointed time.

Footnotes for Chapter Two

1. V. I. Lenin, <u>Collected Works</u>, Vol. 29, Moscow 1974, p. 421.

2. An example of the many issues of contraversy surrounding the analysis of relations of production in the dependent mode of production is the critisism of theorists like Samir Amin, Kay and Emmanuel, who, it is claimed, concentrate too much on unequal relations of trade and the role of merchant capital in dependency rather than on unequal relations of production and the internationalisation of capital and labour. See H. Bernstein, 'Underdevelopment and the Law of Value, a Critique of Kay' in Review of African Political Economy, 6(1976), pp. 51-64.

3. C. Ake, <u>Explanatory Notes on the Political Economy of Africa</u>, in Journal of Modern African Studies, 14, 1(1976).

4. F. Fanon, <u>The Wretched of the Earth</u>, Macgibbon, London 1965.

5. I. G. Shivji, <u>Class Struggle in Tanzania</u>, in Monthly Review Press, London 1976, p. 20.

6. R. H. Green, <u>Political Independence and the National Economy: Essay in the Political Economy of Decolonisation</u>, New York 1975, pp. 273-324.

7. See Issa G. Shivji, op. cit., and Mahmood Mamdani, <u>Politics and Class Formation in Uganda</u>, Monthly Review Press, New York and London 1976.

8. K. Marx and F. Engels, <u>The Communist Manifesto</u>, Monthly Review Press, New York 1968, pp. 45-47.

9. J. Marshall, <u>The State of Ambivalence: Right and Left Options in Ghana</u>, Review of the African Political Economy, 5(1976), pp. 49-62.

10. Gavin Williams, <u>The Social Stratification of a Neo-Colonial Economy: Western Nigerian</u>, in Christopher Allen and R. W. Johnson (eds.), <u>African Perspectives: Papers in the History, Politics and Economics of Africa</u>, Presented to Thomas Hodgkin, Cambridge University Press 1970, pp. 225-50.

11. Issa G. Shivji, op. cit., p. 32.

12. A. Cabral, Revolution in Guinea Bissau, Monthly Review Press, NY, 1969.

13. See Stuart R. Schram, The Political Thought of Mao-Tse-tung, Praeger, N. Y. 1963, pp. 202-64.

14. Issa G. Shivji, op. cit., pp. 22-4 and pp. 116-20.

15. J. Saul, African Peasantries, in J. Daniel, Political Economy of Africa, Longmann, London 1981, p. 114.

16. See Richard Sandbrook and Robin Cohen (eds.), The Development of an African Working Class, Longmann, Kondon 1975.

17. F. Fanon, op. cit. (1965).

18. E. Berg, Major Issues of Wage Policy in Africa, in A. M. Rose (ed.), Industrial Relations and Economic Development, MacMillan, London 1966, cited by C. Allen, Unions, Income and Development, in Development Trends in Kenya, Centre of African Studies, Edinburgh 1972.

19. Egbert Gerken, Arbeitsmärkte in Entwicklungsländern, Kieler Studien 163, 1981, pp. 1-2.

20. K. Hinchcliffe, Labour Aristocracy, A Northern Nigerian Case Study, in Journal of Modern African Studies, 12, 1(1974).

21. Peter Watermann, The Labour Aristocracy in Africa, Introduction to an Unfinished Contraversy, in South African Labour Bulletin, 2, 5(1975), pp. 10-27.

22. G. Arrighi and J. Saul, Essays on the Political Economy of Africa, New York, Monthly Review 1973.

23. P. Msekwa, Workers' Participation in Management in Tanzania, in African Review, 5, 2/1975), p. 131.

24. A. J. Temu, Public Involvement in Planning and Development in Tanzania, Paper presented at the University of York Overseas School, Sept. 1973.

25. TANU Guidelines on Guarding, Consolidating and Advancing the Revolution of Tanzania, and Africa (1972). Clause 15 of these Party Guidelines is on Workers participation in Management: "Together with the issue of involving the people in solving their problems, there is also the question of the habits of leaders in their work and in day-to-day life. There must be a deliberate effort to build equality between

the leaders and those they lead. For a Tanzanian leader it must be forbidden to be arrogant, extravagant, contemptuous and oppressive. The Tanzanian leader has to be a person who respects people, scorns ostentation who is not a tyrant. He should epitomise heroism, bravery, and be a champion of justice and equality. Similarly, the party has the responsibility to fight the vindictiveness of some of its agents, such actions do not promote socialism but drive a wedge between the Party and the government on the one side and the people on the other."

26. P. L. Lawrence, Socialism, Self-Reliance and Foreign Aid in Tanzania. Some Lessons from the Socialist Experience, ERB, UDSM, 1972. Also see P. Mihyo, The Struggle for Workers' Political Control in Tanzania, Review of the African Political Economy, 4(1975), pp. 62-85, and H. Mapolu, The Organisation and Participation of Workers in Tanzania, in African Review 2, 3(1972), pp. 381-415.

27. J. Saul and R. Woods, op. cit., p. 112.

28. H. Bernstein, Concepts for the Analysis of Contemporary Peasantries, in Journal of Peasant Studies, 6, 4(1979), p. 15.

29. Uma Lele, The Design of Rural Development, Lessons from Africa, Baltimore, John Hopkins University Press, 1975, p. 20.

30. Ibid, pp. 14-16.

31. UNO, Paper E/CN.14/CAP.6/2.

32. C. Ake, A Political Economy of Africa, Longman 1981, p. 115.

33. J. Galtung, Integrated Rural Development in Africa, N.Y. 1979

34. H. Mapolu and Philipson, Ujamaa Vijijini, in Africa Development, New York 1981, pp. 7-9.

35. Rosemary Galli (ed.), Political Economy of Rural Development, New York 1981, pp. 7-9.

36. Bruno Musti de Gennaro, Ujamaa: The Aggrandizement of the State, in R. Galli (ed), The Political Economy of Rural Development, N.Y. 1981, p. 111.

37. H. Bernstein, op. cit., p. 16.

38. G. Hyden, "Beyond Ujamaa in Tanzania", Berkeley: University of California Press 1980, pp. 1-18.

39. D. W. Norman, The Organizational Consequences of Social and Economic Constraints and Policies in Dry-Land Areas, Reading, U.K. 1974.

40. J. H. Cleave, African Farmers: Labour Use in the Development of Smallholder Agriculture, N.Y. 1974, p. 34.

41. UN, Economic Commission for Africa, Human Resource Development Division, Women: The Neglected Human Resource for African Development, in Canadian Journal of African Studies, Vol. 6, No. 2, 1972, pp. 359-70.

42. J. H. Cleave, op. cit., pp. 171-73.

43. J. W. Mellor, Agricultural Price Policy and Income Distribution in Africa, Washington, D.C., World Bank, Dec. 1973, p. 29.

44. E. J. Berg, Socialist Ideology and Marketing Policy in Africa, in R. Moyer (ed), Markets and Marketing in Development Economics, Homewood, III., 1978, p. 24.

45. J. Friedrichs, Methoden empirischer Sozialforschung, München 1973, p. 246.

46. Master-Rolls and Work-Cards are files and documents in which the particulars of the labourer in the sisal plantations like name, date of birth, place of birth, tribe, marital status, date of employment etc. are recorded including their distribution in their various sections of the plantation namely cutting the sisal leaves, transport, decortication, brush-room, weeding and nursery etc.

47. G. Payne, Sociology and Social Research, London 1981, p. 61.

48. C. Clark, Basic Economy and Demographic Modules, New York, 1981, p. 13.

49. J. Neil, Economy and Society: A Study in Integration of Economic and Social Theory, Boston 1975, p. 362.

50. D. Katz, Research Methods in Behavioral Sciences, New York 1969, p. 20.

51. K. Ernst, Tradition and Progress in the African Village, New York 1979.

52. D. Freedman, <u>A Multi-Purpose Household Questionnaire</u>, Washington, D.C. 1977, p. 14.

53. T. Weisner, <u>One Family, Two Households: Rural-Urban Network Model of Urbanism</u>, Nairobi 1978, p. 34.

54. Freedman, op. cit., p. 17.

55. For a more detailed discussion of the problem of underutilization of labour see: ILO, <u>Meeting of Experts on Measurement of Underemployment</u>, Working Paper No. 1, Geneva 1973.

56. Throughout the survey the time period taken was the past 12 months, i.e. past year. Sometimes it was difficult for the interviewees to remember about activities of the past year, so the agricultural year was used. The local people in the region call it "Msimu".

57. T. Weisner, op. cit., p. 22.

58. J. M. Due, <u>Costs, Returns and Payments Experience of Ujamaa Villages in Tanzania, 1973-1976</u>, University Press of 1980.

59. H. Menzel (ed.), <u>The Relationship between Individual and Collective Properties</u>, New York 1970, p. 28.

III. THE GENERAL CHARACTERISTICS OF THE TANGA REGION

3.1. Location

Tanga region is located in the north-eastern part of Tanzania, 4°-6° of latitude, north of the equator and 37°-39° 10' of longitude east.
The northern boundary forms the international frontier with Kenya. In the east it is bordered by the Indian Ocean, in the south by the Morogoro and the Coast (Pwani) regions and in the west by the Kilimanjaro and Arusha regions (see Map 3.1).

3.2. Size and Administrative Divisions

The 21 regions of Tanzania range in size from 82,000 sq.kms (Arusha) to 88 sq.kms (Dar es salaam). The average size is 44,200 sq.kms. The Tanga region with 26,807 sq.kms is one of the smallest regions, ranking 16th and representing 3 % of the total land area of the country.[1] Table 3.1 shows the size of the districts and divisions in the region.
The region is divided into six administrative districts: Handeni, Korogwe, Lushoto, Muheza, Pangani and Tanga.
Each district is further divided into divisions (Tarafa) and latter are divided into subdivisions known in Kiswahili language as 'Kata'.

About 75 % of the region or approximately 2 million hectares are suitable for agricultural production, although less than 800,000 hectares are actually used for this purpose.[2]

MAP 3.1   THE LOCATION OF THE TANGA REGION

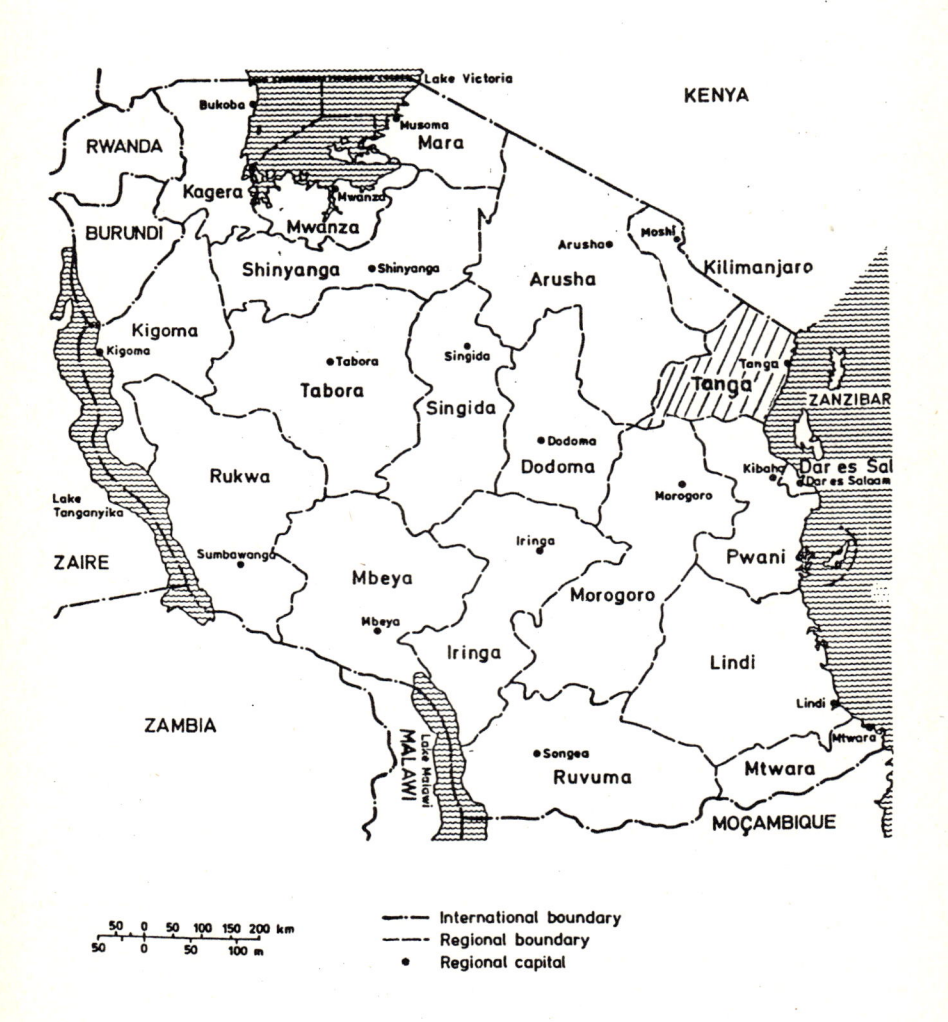

Table 3.1: **Districts and Divisions in Tanga Region (1983)**

District/Division	Area (sq.km)	District/Division	Area (sq.km)
Handeni	13 210	**Muheza** (Tanga Rural)	4 922
Chanika	2 134		
Kimbe	855	Amani	316
Kwamsisi	919	Bwembwera	451
Kwekivu	1 608	Mkinga	1 259
Magamba	1 355	Maramba	1 689
Mazingara	1 083	Muheza	558
Mgera	1 254	Pongwe	549
Mgumburu	910		
Mswaki	2 028	**Pangani**	1 424
Mzundu	2 064	Madanga	287
		Mkwaja	448
Korogwe	3 750	Mwera	589
Bungu	285		
Korogwe	585	**Tanga Town**	
Mombo	2 987		
Magoma	901	**Tanga Region**	26 810
Lushoto	3 497		
Bumbuli	433		
Lushoto	267		
Mlalo	440		
Mlola	451		
Mtae	1 740		
Soni	166		

Source: Survey Department, Dar-es-salaam, 1983

Map 3.2 DISTRICTS OF THE TANGA REGION

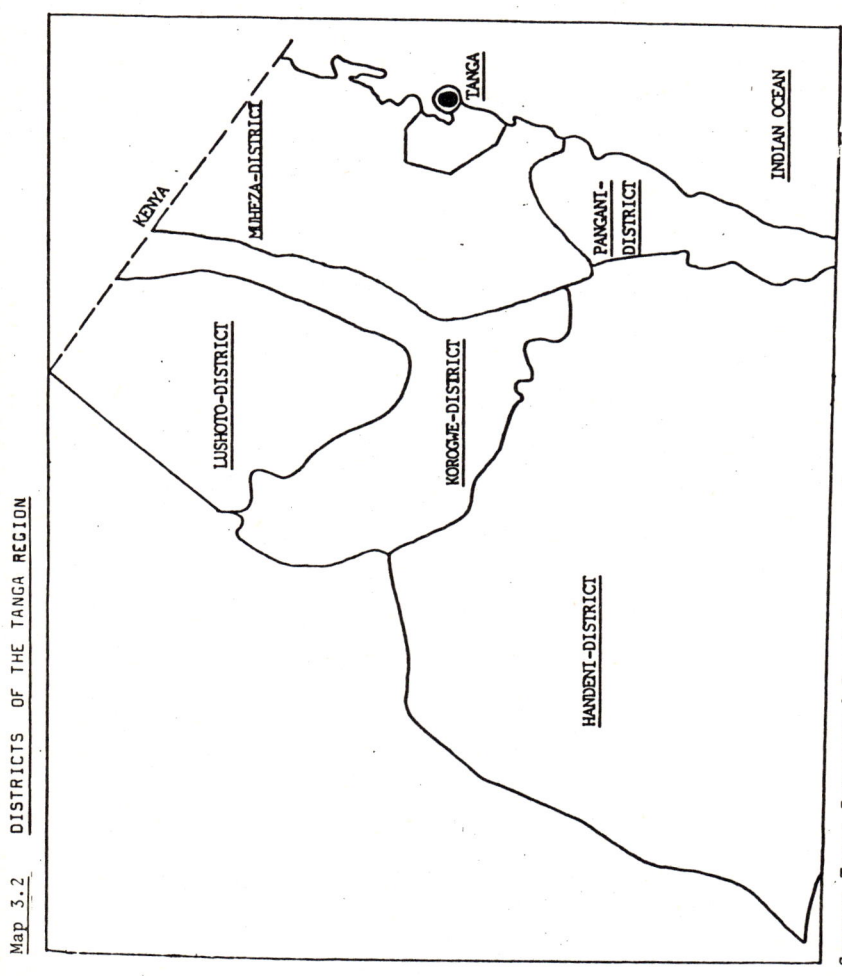

Source: Tanga Integrated Rural Development Programme

3.3. Physiography

Various land forms are present in the Tanga region. The coastal plain extends approximately 60 to 70 kms from the sea shore. In the northern part of the region, the Usambara Mountains rise to a height of 2,400 metres. In the south-west a low level plateau rises gradually some 1,000 metres to the Masai steppe situated in the west. The Masai steppe is bordered on the north by the Nguru Mountains range rising up to 1,500 metres.
The region is also part of the Indian Ocean drainage basin. The most important river in the region is the Pangani river. It rises in the Kilimanjaro Mountain and runs into the Indian Ocean near Pangani town. The other rivers in the region include the Umba, Mkomazi, Sigi (which have perennial discharges), Bombo, Msimbazi, Mkumuzi and Mligaji (with periodical discharges). The areas of the north-west Handeni are without any river.[3]

3.4. Climate

As a result of the various land forms, the region has a wide variation of climate and vegetation. These range from the low rainfall areas of the plains to areas with high rainfall such as Amani and Lushoto in the Usambara Mountains, where large forest areas and intensive small-holder cultivation with a wide variety of crops exist. The dominant climate along the coast and its immediate inland is warm and wet. As a result of the influence of the Indian Ocean there is no large variation of temperature on the coast.

During the hot months (December to March) the average temperature in Tanga town is approximately 30° to 32° C

during the day and about 26° to 29° C at night; during
the cool months (May to October) approximately 23° to
28° C during the day and 20° to 24° C at night.
Another characteristic of the coastal climate is the
high atmospheric humidity, which often rises up to 100 %
maximum. The minimum is about 65 to 70 %.
In the western plateau of Handeni district a hot and
dry climate dominates and in the Usambara Mountains
a temperate climate.

For farming purposes in the region, rainfall is the
most important climatic factor. Mean annual and monthly
rainfall as well as the rainfall probability are of
particular relevance for agricultural activities (see
Map 3.3). These rainfall patterns determine the various
agricultural seasons. There are normally two main rainy
seasons in the region and one period of intermittant
heavy showers may occur:
- short rains (Vuli) - between October and January,
- long rains (Masika) - between Middle of March and
  Mai (they produce about 50 % of the annual total
  precipitation);
- heavy showers (Mchoo) - June or July.

the average amount of precipitation is about 1,100 to
1400 mm along the coast, decreasing further inland.
The important exception from the pattern are the Usambara Mountains where, depending on slope position and
altitude, the amount of precipitation may exceed 2,000 mm.
In the Usambara Mountains the maximum rainfall may be
received after the slackening of the north-east monsoon
winds (i.e. March to May) on north-facing slopes and
after the ending of the south-east monsoon (i.e. October
to December) on south-facing zones. Table 3.2 shows
the average annual rainfall in the district towns of
the region.

Map 3.3 **MEAN ANNUAL RAINFALL AND RAINFALL PROBABILITIES IN TANGA REGION**

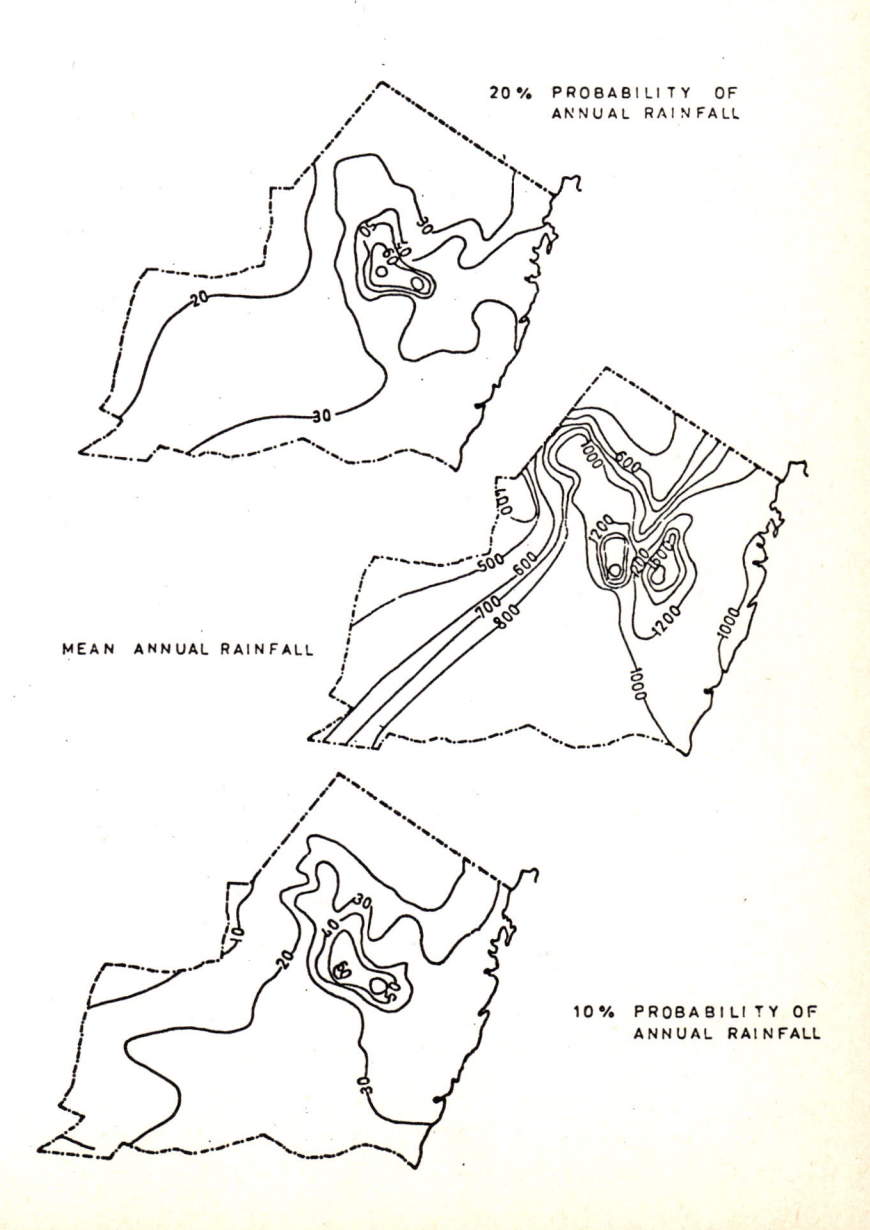

20% PROBABILITY OF ANNUAL RAINFALL

MEAN ANNUAL RAINFALL

10% PROBABILITY OF ANNUAL RAINFALL

Table 3.2: Average Annual Rainfall in the District Towns of the Tanga Region (in mm/year)

District town	Average rainfall	No. of years recorded
Handeni	875	46
Lushoto	1101	53
Korogwe	1097	38
Muheza	1132	8
Pangani	1231	51
Tanga	1356	53

Source: Meterological Department Tanga

In the Masai plains (North-west of Handeni) and in the dry plains of Korogwe district the average precipitation are below 600 mm.
However, an analysis of rainfall is of limited use without reference to the evaporation rates. A rainfall of 750 mm per year is adequate for agriculture in many parts of the world but as a result of the high evaporation rates in Tanzania this figure may mark the limit below which cultivation is marginal. In the Tanga region most areas get at least this minimal amount of rainfall.[4]
Water requirements for agriculture are closely related to the potential evaporation. Potential evaporation tends to decrease with altitude. This reflects the variation of cloud cover with height.[5]

3.5. Population and its structure

Information about the population of an area and its structure in terms of size, distribution, growth rates,

age groups, sex-ratios and social structures is not
only one of the most important production factors but
also a central issue of its development.

The Arusha Declaration of 1967 has envisaged that the
socio-economic development of Tanzania will not depend
on financial resources which the country does not have
but on the abundant resources available. One of them
are its people.[6]

3.5.1. Size and Distribution

In 1978, when a census was taken, the Tanga region had
a population of 1,088,592 people. This was equivalent to 6 %
of the total population of the country. 47.9 % of the
population were women.[7]

Table 3.3 shows the population densities per district.
According to Table 3.3 the inhabitants of Handeni district,
which covers nearly half of the area of the region,
represent only 17 % of the total population of the region,
whereas one third of the region's population is living
in the Lushoto district which covers only 13 % of the
area.

Moreover, with a population density of 13 persons per
sq.km Handeni has about one-third of the region's average.

According to the Census Office in Dar-es-salaam, population
density in the Handeni district is lowest in its Mswaki
division (6 persons per sq.km), which is nearly without
any communication system, and highest in Mgambo (21)
and Chanika (20). the latter is the district headquarters.
This signifies that the highest density in the district
is along the trunk road Korogwe-Chalinze and the Korogwe-
Handeni road.

Table 3.3: Population Density per District (1978)

District	Population	Area in sq.km	Population density/sq.km	Annual growth rates (%)
Lushoto	286069	3497	82	3.7
Korogwe	191115	3756	51	2.2
Muheza	199674	4421	45	2.0
Tanga	143878	500	288	4.8
Pangani	33340	1425	23	2.9
Handeni	184516	13209	14	3.7
Region	1088592	26808	41	2.9

Source: Bureau of Statistics, 1978 Population Census Report

Korogwe district has its highest density in the Bungu division (145) because of the better climatic conditions in the Usambara Mountains where tea is grown. Another division with a high population density is Korogwe (77), where the trunk road Moshi-Tanga-Dar es salaam and the railway Arusha-Moshi-Dar-Tanga runs. Lowest population densities are found in the two dry divisions in the North-west (Mombo Division) with 26 persons per sq.km and in the North-east (Magoma) with 22 persons per sq.km. With a population density of 82 persons per sq.km, the Lushoto district is double the regional average.

However its population density is lower in the dry plains north of the mountains (9). Within the mountains areas, the population density is correlated with the relative accessibility of the different areas as a result of the quality of the road system. It is therefore highest

in the Soni subdivision (295) which lies along the Lushoto-
Mombo road and lowest in Mlola division (69).
In the Muheza district population density is relatively
low in the two northern divisions of Mkinga (27) and
Maramba (30). Along the coast and the foothills of the
Usambara Mountains, the population density rises. The
density of the other divisions is between (55) in Amani
and (90) in Muheza. It is highest near the trunk road
Tanga-Korogwe.

3.5.2. Sex-ratios and Age groups

In order to get the labour force distribution in the
region, the age groups are broken down into four groups:
0-4 years, 5-14 (children of school age), 15-49 (working-
age adults) and those above 49 years of age.

Table 3.4 shows the distribution of the school-age children
and working-age adults as percentages of the total populations in the districts. The table gives also the sex-
ratios; i.e. the number of males per 100 females.
In Handeni and Lushoto, where there are more females
than males, the percentage of children of school-age
is above the regional average, but that of working-
age adults is below the average. In the other districts,
the opposite is the case.

The overall sex-ratio within the districts is affected
by migration. The high sex-ratios of Korogwe, Muheza
and Pangani are based on the quest for employment opportunities. These are the areas with the highest concentration
of sisal estates in search of work. Moreover, migration
is also a search for better natural living conditions
like water, climate and soil fertility. In the Handeni

district, for instance, the low sex-ratio is due to little migration into the district because of its poor natural conditions, such as drought and lack of job opportunities.[8]

Table 3.4: School-age Children and Working-age Adults as Percentages of the Total Population and Sex-ratios in the Districts of the Tanga Region (1979)

District	School-age	People able to work	Sex-ratios in the Districts
Handeni	23.3	40.1	95
Korogwe	19.0	47.0	116
Lushoto	24.7	38.0	87
Muheza	16.3	49.0	122
Pangani	15.7	51.2	123
Tanga	17.0	53.8	119
Region	20.3	44.5	106

Source: Regional Development Directors Office, Tanga

Lushoto has the lowest sex-ratio in the region (87). Here the natural conditions are good, but the area is overpopulated and many men migrate to find job opportunities and land outside the district.[9]

3.5.3. Tribal Groupings and their Socio-economic Structures

Prior to the German colonial incursion, the area which is now the Tanga region formed no single political unit.

It consisted of 'independent' producers still involved in pre-capitalist modes of production,[10] generally clustered in various socio-economic groupings that are normally referred to as 'tribes'.[11]

A general characterization of these groupings is extremely difficult because of the inadequacy and contradictory nature of the available information about them. Nevertheless, two common features can be isolated:
First, the dominant productive system was the village community consisting of small peasant cultivators. Second, they belong to the Bantu group of African languages, which means that their languages were related. There were two types of Bantu groups in the area at the time. The so-called old Bantu, like the Zigua, Shambaa and Bondei, and the young Bantus, who include the Digo and the Segeju people. The former arrived in the area before the latter. Traditionally they varied in size, social and political structures.[12]

Below we shall try to examine the social organisations of these tribal groupings by concentrating on the traditional inhabitants of three districts of the region which have been previously studied and about which information is accessible, i.e. the Zigua people in Handeni and certain parts of the Korogwe district, and the Shambaa in the Korogwe and Lushoto districts.

3.5.3.1. The Zigua

3.5.3.1.1. Distribution

Traditionally the Zigua people lived in Uzigua, Unguu (present day Handeni district) and the Pangani Valley in the Mafi area from the base of the Usambara Mountains as far as the Mkomazi River (North-western part of the Korogwe district).[13]

Today the Zigua are found in the different parts of the Tanga region and Tanzania at large engaged in different socio-economic activities. According to the population census of 1978,. there are 233,764 Zigua people in Tanzania mainland. 183,644 of them are distributed in the various parts of the Tanga region and form about 97 % of the total population of the Handeni district,[14] which leads to the tribal homogeneity of the district.

3.5.3.1.2. Economic Activities

The Zigua in the Handeni district are crop cultivators and pastoralists.[15] The traditional agricultural crops are sorghum, millet, and tobacco, with the first two being the main staple food crops before the British introduced maize and cassava. The latter is a famine crop. The German introduction of cotton as a cash crop for the peasant farmers resulted from the desire to levy taxes upon the inhabitants, as well as from the search for raw materials for the industrial needs of the colonial countries.[16] Before the colonial establishment in the late 1880s, the growing of bananas, coconuts, tomatoes and other vegetables were introduced into the fertile areas of eastern Handeni through trading relations with the coastal people, i.e. with Arabs, Swahili and Indians.[17]

The average size of the farms per family is about 1/2 to 1 hectare. The hoe and cutlass are the main instruments of labour. Fertilizers, both natural and artificial

are not common.[18]
The type of livestock kept are cattle, goats, sheep and chicken, with the size of the herds depending on the well-being of the family. There are people who own no livestock at all, whereas others have more than thirty herds of cattle, goats or sheep.[19] Goats, sheep and chicken are common in all parts of the district with cattle being mostly found in large numbers in the Northwestern parts.[20]

Like in other tribal groups of the country where animal husbandry is present, livestock has a multiple value and represents in varying degrees a store of wealth, a sign of prestige, prerequisite of marriage or parenthood.

Different types of livestock are kept for different reasons: Cattle are considered as an item of property, while sheep and goats are more of a commercial value. The animals are only slaughtered on special occasions such as rituals and festivities.[21] The main problem which is still affecting the socio-economic development of the Zigua people in Handeni is lack of water for domestic purposes and for their crops and animals. The rains are unreliable and there are frequent periods of drought.[22]
The agricultural prosperity of the area which Oskar Baumann observed during his travels through the area might have been in the short periods of good rains.[23]

In the traditional villages, animal husbandry and crop cultivation was done in cooperation, even though the animals and fields were privately owned. There was a system of looking after the animals, especially the cattle, by a rotation of the elders of the village.

Young boys and girls were given the task of caring for sheep and goats. In crop cultivation, it was common for a peasant farmer to invite the assistance of his fellow villagers usually clan members to help him overcome certain labour peaks in return for food and drink. This system is known as 'Chiwili'.[24] However, with the restructuring of the old villages and the formation of new villages under government directives, the system of 'Chiwili' is losing its traditional form of reciprocity. It is now normal in the new villages for the well-to-do peasants to employ wage labour.[25]

3.5.3.1.3. Housing Patterns

The traditional villages of the Zigua people are composed of 10 to 200 round huts commonly known in Kiswahili as 'Msonge', with small windows, usually one for each hut. The huts were plastered with mud or cowdung. Each village had an enclosure made of thorny trees with a gate.[26] The purpose for the enclosure was to control the unwanted intrusion of strangers, especially the Masai, who stole their cattle, and later the colonial tax collectors and cotton extension officers. The enclosures can still be seen in some of the villages which have not yet been integrated in the new villages established during the 'Ujamaa movement'. In the new villages the houses are a mixture of the old round huts adjacent to spacious 'modern' rectangular houses. Some of the latter houses have iron-roofs and cemented floors.[27]

The traditional huts were divided inside into different parts: On the outside part of the hut was a small room where the wooden motar was kept. The inner rooms were divided as follows: to the right of the entrance wood was kept; to the left stayed the animals (goats or sheep) tied to a small wood; on one part was the family store where the baskets were kept. At the middle was the fire place. The people slept near the fire place. The cattle stayed outside in the enclosure or 'Boma'.[28] The modern houses reflect the prosperity of the owners.

3.5.3.1.4. Pre-Colonial Kinship Relations

The political and economic developments of the past decades have greatly affected the traditional forms of social organisations of the Zigua and other tribal groups in the region.[29] Traditionally the Zigua are matrilineal people, i.e. importance is placed on the mothers' side of clan relatives.[30] The Zigua are said to have been composed of 50 to 80 matriclans.[31] Each clan occupied a certain area and had a number of matrilineages or 'Milango'.[32] The clan and area took the name of the dominant 'Mlango'. The clans which shared common boundaries were socially connected by joking relations called 'Utani'. The word 'Utani' came from the Arab word 'Watana' meaning people who are familiar to each other. These relations formed what is known among the Wazigua as 'Lukolo'.[33]

The leader of the dominant matrilineage was the chief of the clan and its spiritual leader. His position was inherited not by his sons but his nephew (the son of his sister). However, as a result of political changes which first came with colonialization, the political structure of the matrilineages has lost its traditional significance. The German colonial government replaced the traditional chiefs with administrative officials recruited from the coastal areas 'the Akidas'.

On the other hand, the British administration with its
system of 'indirect rule' reinstated the chiefs with
a new responsibility of enforcing colonial policies -
especially the collection of tax and cultivation of
cotton.[34] This made the chiefs unpopular among their
own people.[35]

Moreover, the destruction of the structure of matrilineages has led to the development of the emphasis
on independent family units. The authority of the father
is now becoming dominant in the family affairs rather
than that of the uncle. The latter has still power
over his nephews and has to be consulted in all the
family activities concerning them.[36]

3.5.3.1.5. Marriage Relationships

An early marriage engagement for young girls was common
among the Zigua people. All girls in the age between
eight and ten years were required to participate in
the 'Mkinda-rite' as a preparation for marriage. In eth-
nological literature[37] it is shown that it was during
this rite that the girls were circumcised. After this
ceremony the girls were ready for marriage.[38]

During the engagement period the young man had to spend
a portion of his time in the village of his future in-
laws helping them with a number of activities which
included farm work. He was usually accompanied by his
friends. The activities became more intensive after
marriage and helped to reduce the dowry for the bride.
After marriage the married man lived in the village
of his in-laws.[39] There is no exact information as regards
the length of the time the man must live in the village
of his in-laws before being able to return to his own

village.
It is sometimes argued that he could return after the
birth of the first child, or three to four years after
the marriage.

Today the engagement of young girls from ten or eleven
years of age is discouraged by the government and because
of formal education very few girls do take part in the
'Mkinda rites'. Moreover, the dowry for the bride is
now paid in form of money and the married man is not required to live in the village of his in-laws and work them.
For the married woman these new changes mean that contact
with her family members has been diminished. Before a
man divorced his wife, the family of the latter had to
be consulted, and if the man is responsible for the divorce
the dowry was not returned. This was also the case if
the couple had children.[40]
There is no exact information concerning with whom the
children remain after a marriage has broken down. According to a research made by McVicars on the Zigua traditions,
the children remain with the mother.[41] But other sources
of information argue that there is no constant rule
with respect to this issue. The boys could remain with
the father and the girls with the mother or they could
all remain with any one of the two parents. There are
cases in which women took care of their children depending
on their income from agriculture and petty trades.[42]

3.5.3.1.6. Division of Labour

As regards the division of labour between man and wife,
the husband was responsible for hunting, looking after
the cattle, taking care of the strenuous activities
in crop cultivation such as cutting trees, digging water

channels, protecting the household and property, including crops in the farm, especially during the night.
The wife's activities included cooking, taking care of children, cleaning of the house, collecting firewood and water, weeding and harvesting the garden and other daily activities on the farm. Pottery and braiding were also traditionally the activities of women.[43]
The man was responsible for the control of the family income and there is general agreement among the different sources of information that most men decided themselves about the utilization of the income without consulting their wives. This tendency still exists.[44]

3.5.3.1.7. Religions

The 1978 population census showed that 4/5 of the population of Handeni district was composed of muslims.[45] Islam in the area came through trading relations with Arabs and Swahili people from the coast before the time of colonial establishment. Another historical experience which contributed to the contact between the Zigua and the coastal peoples was the famine of 1836 which caused a number of the Zigua people to move to the coast in search of food, and some are said to have offered themselves to the Arabs as slaves.[46] Moreover, during the German colonial period most of the administrative officials (the Akidas) who worked in the interior of Tanga, were muslims recruited from the coast.[47]

The few christians who are in the district are divided between those belonging to the Anglican Universities Missions to Central Africa (UMCA), the church Missionary Society (CMS) and the Holy Fathers of the Catholic Church. The UMCA christians are mostly in the North-east, including some parts of Korogwe and the central parts of Handeni.

In 1867 the UMCA missionaries established themselves
for the first time at Magila in the present day Muheza
district. Coming from Zanzibar, they established several
stations in the various parts of the region, including
Zigualand. Being British, their activities were limited
by the contradictions between the Germans and the British,
especially during the German colonial period.
They became active again after the defeat of the Germans
in the First World War.

In 1931 they had already established churches in different
parts of Handeni, including Kwamkono, Kwamazi, Mandera,
Ngugwini, Sangeni and King'ombe. They also introduced
formal education into these areas for their converts.[48]

The Church Missionary Society had its influence in Western
parts of the district. Its activities were also halted
during the First World War and reopened after. Its main
area of activities were in the present day Kwekivu division, which includes Songe, Masagula, Tunguli and
Gingi.[49]

The Catholic Fathers' activities startet at the end
of the 19th century along the coast neighbouring Zigualand. They had no great influence in the district because
of the already established muslim religion in its areas
of operation. Their only station in the area was built
in 1931 at Kwadiboma in Ngulu and was rebuilt by the
Italian Rosminian Order in 1953. Other small areas of
catholic influence were established at Vyadigwa, Lulago
and Korudiga.

Traditional beliefs exist also within the areas of both
Islam and Christianity. In the traditional beliefs

emphasis is placed on the ancestors of different clans
who are founders of the respective clans. Sacrifices
are made to them by individuals, families or clan members. These are expressions of thank, intercession or
conciliation. Besides the worship of ancestors, the
Zigua people, like the other tribal groups in the region,
believe in a higher power than man to whom they ascribe
different names 'Mulungu' (God), 'Chohile' (Justice)
or 'Matelenganya' (performer of wonders). They also
sacrifice to him for his favours.[50]

3.5.3.2. The Shambaa

3.5.3.2.1. Distribution and Economic Activities

There are about 346,069 Shambaa people in mainland Tanzania. 326,960 of them are scattered throughout different
parts of the Tanga region, but more than 85 % of them
live in the Usambara Mountains which include most of
the Lushoto district and some parts of Korogwe.[51]
The Shambaa are traditionally an agricultural people,
who according to Murdock[52] belong to the Bantu highland
farmers - together with the Chagga, Kamba, Kikuyu, Meru,
Pare and Taita.

In the Shambaa language, the final 'i' signifies the
locative case. Thus, the Shambaa are the people living
in 'Shambaai'. 'Shambaai' also describes a specific
ecological entity - mountainous environment whose characteristics have formed the Shambaa culture and have also
been formed by this culture.[53] This corresponds to
Boesch's[54] term "biotop", defining an environment where
man adapts his activities to the conditions of the environment (accomodation) and actively changes specific
characteristics of that environment according to his

needs (assimilation). Altitude, temperature, soil, and
rainfall of the Usambaras favour certain vegetation
and specific ways of planting. In their adaptation process the Shambaa had to detect all the characteristics
of this environment. In addition to this accomodation,
an assimilation process also took place: the people
adapted plants to the local conditions, discovered new
varieties of food crops, and thus gradually changed
the vegetation of the Usambaras.[55] Before the introduction
of coffee and tea by colonialism, the main agricultural
crops in the Usambaras were bananas, beans, peas, maize,
sweet potatoes, yams, tomatoes, pepper, sugar cane and
tobacco.
Bananas were found almost throughout the Usambaras.
Near the huts were banana and tobacco fields. Although
some tobacco was traded with the coastal people, most
of it was used locally. In preparation of the tobacco,
the leaves were dried, then mixed with water. They were
later pounded on a wooden motor, left for a period of
time and later formed into cakes which were left to
dry. When someone wanted to smoke, he cut a slice of
it. The same technology of preparing tobacco for local
use is still being used in some parts. Beer was made
out of sugar cane and maize.

The fight for survival has led some Shambaa periodically
to farming in areas outside the 'Shambaai' (called in
the Shambaa language "nyika") because of differences
in growing times of certain food crops at different
altitudes. Feierman reports that in areas like Vuga,
maize grown from March to May could be harvested in
'nyika' in July but in Shambaai, not until September
or October. By planting in Shambaai and 'nyika', the
peasant farmers of Vuga living on the edge of the Usambaras considerably shortened the time between harvests,
thus ensuring additional security.

In western Usambara, especially the southern parts like
Vugiri and Kwambugu, animal husbandry was practised.
The common animals kept were cattle, sheep, goats and
chicken.
Two types of communal work were practised among the
Shambaa:
(i) 'kuimiana, where either a man or woman received
assistance from one or two others by deciding to
take turns working in the fields, without giving
any kind of payment;
(ii) 'ngemo' where members of a clan, neighbours, in-
laws and friends provided assistance. The helpers
were not paid but received a good meal and sometimes
drinks as well.

After the field has been cleared, the women were responsible for planting, harrowing and weeding. The husband's
responsibility lies with the 'fields of the man' (mashamba
ya kighoshi), such as tobacco and coffee or tea fields.
His work involves caring for the fields by carrying
out the work necessary for the type of crop and weather
conditions. The husbands advantage over the woman is
that he could order all the other members of the household to work in his fields. The wife on the other hand
could not be sure of her husband's assistance. For instance, if social obligations such as funeral ceremonies
conflicted with the husband's farming duties, she had
to work alone or with some of her children.[56]

Working in the fields played an important role in the
area of communication and discourse. For instance a
family on its way to the field passed not only the land
in the vicinity of their hamlets but also a number of
other hamlets.
They might see a farmer planting a new variety of

vegetables, or another using some type of manure previously unknown to the people in their own hamlet. They could stop to talk with other farmers about their experiences with their particular fields and crops. Passing one of the hamlets, they might meet friends or relatives and use the occasion to chat, thus exchanging the latest news. Communal farming brought together people from different hamlets and even villages and also contributed to the enlargement of communication possibilities.[57]

3.5.3.2.2. Traditional and 'Modern' Village Patterns

A foreigner travelling to Shambaai today on the road from Mombo to Lushoto passes numerous settlements scattered on the mountain slopes and containing anywhere from 5 to 40 huts. Some huts are round like those of the traditional Zigua people, but most of them are rectangular.
No clear-cut frontiers separate the different villages. Thereby allowing a given hamlet to belong to one or the other village. Communal identity of one village from another is established by either administrative or social rules.[58] The numerous hamlets however differ in a variety of other aspects: The first aspect differentiates between the 'modern' hamlets and the traditional ones, and those with a high proportion of non-farming activities and those where mixed farming activities is the sole source of income. The 'modern' hamlets are characterised by a higher percentage of families whose male members are either employees or independent businessmen outside agriculture and where because of additional income provided by non-farming activities, 'modern' houses with cement floors and iron roofs are numerous.

In the traditional hamlets the only source of income
is mixed farming. The people keep a few cattle and sheep
and rely on coffee, tea or wattle as a cash crop.
The second differentiating factor of the hamlets, although not so revealing as the first, is based on religion - mainly between the muslims and the christians.
Islam was introduced in the Usambaras through trading
relations with the coastal people, whereas christianity
was established by the German protestant missionaries
of the Bethel-Mission. Their first stations were at
Mlalo (1891), Vuga (1895), Bumbuli (1899) and Bungu
(1903).[59]

A study made by Hermann Schönmeier showing the distribution of christian and muslim families in the hamlets
of an area in the Usambaras called Shashui gives the
following interesting information about the followers
of the two religions: He first shows how religious affiliation has an influence on the level of formal education
in the hamlets, especially in respect to women. In the
hamlets of Bagai and Mazukizi, where 44 % and 70 % respectively of the families were christians, 23 % and
50 % respectively of the women had primary education;
whereas in the predominantly Islamic hamlets of Mlangi
(86 %) and Vuli (97 %) only 5 % and 18 % of the women
had primary education. The low figures for the muslim
women with formal education reflects the minor importance
attached to women's education in islamic societies.
He also shows that the percentage of christians working
in an area other than farming was higher than that for
muslims. In the case of the Shashui area it was 21.2 %
to 16.8 %.

Another important aspect pointed out by Schönmeier's
study is the difference in the type of non-agricultural

work done by the two groups of people. The christians
are interested in employment, however not necessarily
self-employment: 18.8 % to 2.4 % self-employed. The
respective figures for Muslims were 8.6 % to 8.0 %.
A possible explanation for this may be that because
of higher level of education and European missionary
influence, christians have more opportunities for office
jobs and crafts. Non-christians are commercially oriented.

3.5.3.2.3. Pre-Colonial Kinship Relations

The social, economic and spiritual life of the Shambaa
people was reflected by certain observations and rites
which involved the family, clan, marriage, youthhood,
blood friendship, slavery, adoption and death. These
relationships were expressed in different proverbs,
property rights, family, kinship and marriage procedures.

The Shambaa are a patrilineal people, i.e. the family
rites mean the rites of the father and his line of relatives.
The father had full rights over his children through
the payment of the dowry. When a man has paid the dowry,
the children from the marriage then belong to his relatives,
especially his male relatives.
When he has no male relatives, they belong to his sister.
When he has no relatives at all, then the rights to
the children will go to the brother of his wife.

When a man has not paid the dowry, the children belonged
to his in-laws until he paid for them. Marriage to many
wives was common among the Shambaa. This depicted the
wealth of the man by showing that he had a lot of goats

for the required dowries. Moreover, many wives also
showed that he had enough land to cultivate, since each
wife had her own hut, household and her own farm. She
was not expected to be an economic burden to her husband.
A man not only had to give enough land to his wife to
be able to support herself and the children, but also
had to acquire wealth. In Shambaai it was a woman's
duty to care for daily needs, and a man's duty to acquire
wealth either by providing the bridewealth for his sons,
meeting the fees of local doctors or by purchasing food
in years of famine. Through their wealth, normally in
the form of cattle and sheep, a family provided for
those situations which surpassed the economic means
of a single farmer.
If, for instance, a member of the family injured a member
of another clan, a compensation had to be paid. In order
to ensure that the compensation was paid it was not
the individual person, but his whole family which was
held responsible.

Traditionally the Shambaa had a lot of kinship relationships. Kinship was based on the following: a common
ancestor's name, the area of origin or certain animals
eaten.
Those based on common animals eaten are: cockchafer
eaters ('Waja nkobo'), crebs dancers ('Wavina nkala'),
gazelle dancers ('Wavina mpala') and monkey dancers
('Wavina kima').
Kinships based on common ancestors: Wankimai, Wataita,
Wahala and Wambugu. Those based on common area of origin:
Walwandai, Wasungwi, Wakilindi and Washele.
The same kinship performs the same sacrifice to the
ancestors, and each family belonged to a certain kinship.
The members of the different kinship groups could marry
without barriers and each could attend his wife's or
her husband's ancestral sacrifices.[60]

3.5.3.2.3.1. Social Differentiation

According to Shambaa tradition, a person had the right to a piece of land as long as he needed it. Land was acquired either through buying it or borrowing it or as a gift from the chief. The value of the land depended on its quality, i.e. whether it was already cleared or not. Before the European penetration, there was no ownership of trees. Fruit trees were introduced by German settlers. The trees which were indigenous were used for building and firewood.[61]

In Shambaai a man who ventured into a new area had the right to the land there. He could give it to anyone he pleased, normally in order to form coalitions which might be helpful against enemy attack. After his death, non-family members retained any land they had been given. During his funeral ceremonies the rights to the land he had given other members of his family were also confirmed. If one of his wives had no sons, her land together with the land not yet allocated was distributed equally between his sons. If they were too young, one of the man's brothers would marry his widow, receive land, and take over the responsibility of raising the children and the later provide the sons with farmland. A daughter could be left farmland if the deceased had enough. This land would be returned to her brothers if, due to marriage, she left the area. If she remained in the area she could keep it and bequeath it to her sons. If she had none, the land would be returned to her family upon her death, since her husband or daughters had no right to it. Farmland received within the family could not be sold, as it was not individual, but common property. In addition to this clan or family land there was free land, which a man could acquire simply by clearing it. This land was viewed as individual property and could be sold.

Water reservoirs for irrigation were a common feature. These were privately owned and the owner had the rights to it and any one who wanted to use the water had to pay a hen to the owner. Private property, such as land, products etc., were protected by charms. The charms were made by special magicians on the farm by laying a horn or pot with certain magical mixtures. The effects of the charms on the expected criminal were different, which included bodily pains, nose bleeding, snake bites etc.[62]

Among the Shambaa there was 'full' slavery and slavery based on 'security'. Exemple of the latter occured when someone could not pay his debts and offered himself to someone who could pay for him. Some people offered themselves to their rich neighbours because of their own poverty. Some parents offered their children to chiefs or rich people because they could not maintain them. When the poverty was over, they took them back. The slaves lived in his village or that of his master, and the master was responsible for the life of his slave. If the latter wanted to get married, the master had to pay his dowry. The children of the slave belonged to his master.[63]

The ruling nobility in the Usambara Mountains was the Kilindi clan. The clan had its origins about 150 years ago in Kilindiland in the land of the Zigua people through their ancestor called Mbega. Their rule was manifested through judicial and administrative officials (Wafungwa), assessors (Watawa), medicinemen (Wag'anga) and blacksmiths (Washilagi).

The administrators were appointed by the Kilindi chief.
The medicinemen and blacksmiths came from special families
of the different clans. The medicinemen were the doctors
of the people. They cured by using charms and incartations
which were believed to protect one against witchcraft.
They banished epidemics and angry spirits beyond the
frontiers of the village and the land.

The chief had the power of life and death over his subjects. Every chief had his confidant called 'Mshaka
mali', who informed him of mistrusts of his subjects.
Around the chief gathered the administrators headed
by the 'Mdoe'. The latter lived in the chief's residence
or 'Kitala' and his farms were also cultivated by the
subjects. The chief decided the public affairs in contact
with his administrators whom he appointed and dismissed.
The Kilindi rule, like all other chiefdoms in Tanzania,
was abolished after independence. The villages are now
under village councils and the Village Party Chairmen
who are elected by the villagers themselves.[64]

3.5.3.3. Other Tribal Groups

The Digo and Segeju in the coastal area traditionally
lived in permanent villages based on the coconut economy
with some subsistance food crops production and fishery.
Cassava was the main staple food because of its drought
resistance nature. Oskar Baumann described them as recent
converts from cattle keepers to crop cultivation due
to Masai raids.[65]

Power was based on age and the number of coconut trees
one had. Young men could only achieve wealth and prestige
through hard labour for the elders until their own trees

were grown.

In the period preceeding colonial rule the societies of the Digo and Segeju were influenced by Arabs who had settled on the coast and intermingled with the local inhabitants. The Arabs were primarily merchants and middle men exporting ivory, food crops and slaves from the interior to Zanzibar.[66]

The common types of Arabs along the Tanga coast during the time were the Maskata and Hadratmant, or 'Shihiri' as they are commonly known by the local people. They established sugar cane and coconut plantations using slave labour. The Digo and Segeju adopted the Arab culture, including technology, religion and kept domestic slaves brought from the interior. As a result of this influence, the freemen among the Digo and Segeju had little inclination to do agricultural work and cultivation of the soil became the work of the slaves. They were engaged also in trade, fishing and handcrafts such as blacksmithing, rope making and pottery.[67]

By prohibiting the slave trade and redirecting the products of the interior to other harbours such as Dar es salaam which served the traffic to Europe, the German colonial administration destroyed the socio-economic basis of the coastal people. The Arab settlements gradually decayed and their plantations were abandoned. The Digo and Segeju were also affected by these changes. They lost some of their old customers and trading partners and their handcraft-products were pushed aside by European imports. They lost their slaves who were integrated into the households in which they worked.[68]

The introduction of sisal plantations in the region brought other tribal groups from as far as Ruvuma, Kigoma,

Mtwara, Zambia, Ruanda and Burundi. These were recruited as labourers, especially during the days of the Sisal Labour Bureau (1944-1965). While the migrant labourers planned to stay for only a few years in the plantations, they finally settled permanently in the area.[69]

3.6. Summary

The purpose of this Chapter was to present the general characteristics of the Tanga region. This overview of the region is significant because it helps the reader to comprehend the aspects analysed in the rest of the study.

The region is located in the north-eastern part of Tanzania. It is one of the smallest regions in the country, covering 3 % of the total area of the country. Less than 0.04 % of the suitable land for agriculture is utilised. There are six administrative districts: Handeni, Korogwe, Muheza, Pangani and Tanga.

Various land forms are present in the region as a result of which the region has a wide variation of climates and vegetation. For farming purposes in the region rainfall is the most important climatic factor. Water requirements for agriculture are closely related to the potential evaporation. The latter tends to decrease with altitude. This reflects the variation of cloud cover with height.

According to the population census of 1978, the Tanga region had 6 % of the total population of the country. 47.9 % of them were women. Although the Handeni district covers nearly half of the area of the region, it has only 17 % of the total population. This is due to poor

climatic conditions. It is the driest district in the
region. About one third of the population of the region
lives in the Lushoto district which includes the Usambara
Mountains. The district covers only 13 % of the regional
area.

The labour force distribution in the region was made
by examining the age groups and sex-ratios. In Handeni
and Lushoto, there are more females than males, and the
percentage of children below 15 years old is above the
regional average. The overall age group and sex-ratio
distributions among the districts are affected by migration.
Migration is in search of employment opportunities,
better natural conditions like water, climate and soil
fertility. In Handeni the low sex ratio is due to little
migration into the district. This is due to its poor
natural conditions and lack of job opportunities. Lushoto
district has the lowest sex-ratio in the region, i.e.
the number of males per 100 females. This is because
the natural conditions are good in the district but
the area is overpopulated. Many men migrate to other
areas to look for employment opportunities and land.

The traditional tribal groupings in the region are the
Zigua, Shambaa, Bondei, Digo and Segeju. All the five
groups belong to the Bantu group of African languages,
which means that their languages are somewhat related.
Traditionally the Zigua live in Handeni and some parts
of Korogwe district; Shambaa in Lushoto and some parts
of Korogwe; Bondei in Muheza; the Digo and Segeju in
the Tanga district.
The tribes live in different ecological areas hence
the crops grown are also different. The traditional
crops of the Zigua are sorghum, millet and tobacco.
The first two were the main staple food crops. The Germans

introduced cotton in the area as a cash crop and the
British introduced maize and cassava. The latter being
a famine crop. The Zigua are also pastoralists.
The Zigua are a matrilineal people, i.e. importance
is placed on the mother's side of the clan relations.
The population census of 1978 showed that 4/5 of the
population of Handeni district were Muslims. Islam came
into the area through trading relations with Arabs and
Swahili people from the coast.

Before the introduction of coffee and tea by colonialism,
the main agricultural crops of the Shambaa were bananas,
beans, peas, maize, sweet potatoes, yams sugar cane
and tobacco. The Shambaa and Bondei are patrilineal
people, i.e. the family rites mean the rites of the
father and his line of relatives.

The Digo and Segeju in the coastal area are recent converts from cattle keepers due to Masai raids. Cassava
is the main food crop and coconuts are a sorce of cash.
The Digo and Segeju have been very much influenced by
Arabs who settled along the coast before colonial establishment. They adopted Arab culture, which includes
technology and religion.

The introduction of sisal plantations in the region
by colonialism brought other tribal groups from outside
the region. These were recruited as labourers, especially
during the days of the Sisal Labour Bureau which had
its recruiting operations in Lindi, Ruvuma, Mtwara,
Kigoma etc. While the migrant labourers planned to stay
for only a few years in the plantations, they finally
settled permanently in the area.

Footnotes for Chapter Three

1. TIRDEP, Tanga Regional Development Plan, 1975-1980, Tanga, May 1975, p. 13.

2. Data collected from the Regional Agricultural Development Office, Tanga.

3. The geographical description of the region is based on information from the Tanga Integrated Rural Development Programme (TIRDEP), Regional Development Plan 1975-1980, pp. 25.26.

4. GTZ, Lower Mkomazi Irrigation Project, Tanzania Feasibility Study, Main Report, Eschborn, FRG, January 1981, pp. 47-48.

5. TIRDEP, op. cit., p. 27.

6. J. K. Nyerere, Arusha Declaration, DSM, p. 3.

7. Bureau of Statistics, 1978 Population Census Report, DSM 1979, p. 38.

8. TIRDEP, op. cit., pp. 24-26.

9. GTZ, op. cit., p. 63.

10. J. Rweyemamu, Underdevelopment and Industrialization in Tanzania, A Study of Perverse Capitalist Industrial Development, Oxofrd University Press, Nairobi and London 1973, p. 3.

11. For definition of the notion 'tribe' see Eduard Sagarin (ed.), Sociology, The Basic Concepts, Holt, Reinehart and Winston, New York 1978, p. 102, and also see Clifford Geerth (ed.), Old Societies and New States, The Quest for modernity in Africa, 1968, p. 168.

12. C. M. Doke, Bantu Modern Grammatik Phonetic and Lexicographical Studies since 1860, IAI, 1967.

13. K. Garrger, Tangaland und die Kolonisation Deutsch-Ostafrika - Thatsachen und Vorschläge, Berlin 1891, pp. 16-17.

14. Bureau of Statistics, 1978 Population Census, DSM, 1979.

15. Elisabeth Grohs, Kisazi, Reiferiten der Mädchen bei den Zigua und Ngulu Ost-Tanzanias, Dietrich Reimer Verlag 1977, p. 29.

16. Michaela von Freyhold, Ujama Villages in Tanzania, An Analysis of a Social Experiment, Heinemann, London 1979, p. 15.

17. Interview with the District Development Agricultural Officer, Handeni, on 25/3/1983.

18. Elisabeth Grohs, op. cit., p. 29.

19. Interview with the District Agricultural Development Officer, Handeni.

20. Elisabeth Grohs, op. cit., p. 30.

21. GTZ, op. cit., p. 8.

22. Elisabeth Grohs, op. cit., p. 31.

23. Oskar Baumann, Usambara und seine Nachbargebiete, Berlin 1891, p. 271.

24. E. Grohs, op. cit., p. 32.

25. GTZ, op. cit., p. 63.

26. E. Grohs, op. cit., p. 32.

27. Interviews with 'Wazee' Omari Mbelwa (Mkalamo village, Korogwe district), Salim Maramba (Sindeni village, Handeni), and Bakari Samadebe (Mkuyu village, Handeni). 'mzee' is a Kiswahili word for old man and 'Wazee' is its plural form. All old people are addressed with this word.

28. E. Grohs, op. cit., p. 40.

29. Ibid.

30. T. O. Beidelmann, Matrilineal Peoples of Eastern Tanzania, London, IAI, 1967.

31. E. Grohs, op. cit., p. 41.

32. The word 'Mlango' in Kiswahili means a door, but in this context it means a group of relatives from ones mother's clan.

33. D. Brokensha, Handeni Revisited, in Arican Affairs, Vol. 70, No. 279, April 1970, p. 22.

34. T. McVicar, The Relations between Religion and Morality among the Wazigua, in Primitive Man, 1, 1939, pp. 105-106.

35. Michaela von Freyhold, *The Potentials for Ujamaa in Handeni. Some Ecological and Historical Characteristics of the District*, DSM, 1972, p. 7.

36. E. Grohs, op. cit., p. 42.

37. H. C. Baxter, *Religious Practices of the Pagan Wazigua*, in TNR, 15, 1954, p. 49-57; also see A. Mokiwa, *Habari za Wazigua*, London 1954, p. 15.

38. Interview with Wazee Omari Mbelwa and Salim Mdimu (Mkalamo).

39. T. McVicar, op. cit., p. 17.

40. E. Grohs, op. cit., pp. 43-45.

41. T. McVicar, op. cit., p. 18.

42. Interview with Wazee Omari Mbelwa and Salimi Mdimu.

43. E. Grohs, op. cit., p. 45.

44. Interview with Wazee Ali Samaguni and Saidi Mvumo (Kimbe).

45. Bureau of Statistics, *1978 Population Census*, DSM, 1979, p. 6.

46. E. A. Alpers, *The Coast and the Development of Caravan Trade*, in I. Kimambo and A. Temu. *A History of Tanzania*, Nairobi 1969, pp. 34-57.

47. S. Feierman, *The Shambaa Kingdom, A History*, Wisconsin 1974, p. 137.

48. A. E. M. Anderson-Morshead, *The History of the UMCA, 1857-1909*, Vol. 1, London 1955, p. 74.

49. E. Grohs, op. cit., pp. 37-38.

50. T. McVicar, *Wanguru Religions*, in Primitive Man, 14, 1941, pp. 13-31.

51. Bureau of Statistics, op. cit., p. 42.

52. G. P. Murdock, *Africa, Its Peoples and Their Culture*, New York and Toronto 1959, p. 342.

53. H. W. Schönmeier, *Agriculture in Conflict, The Shambaa Case*, Kübel Foundation Bensheim 1977, p. 34.

54. E. E. Boesch, Kultur und Biotop, Saarbrücken 1975.
55. H. W. Schönmeier, op. cit., p. 34.
56. S. Feierman, op. cit., pp. 18-31.
57. H. W. Schönmeier, op. cit., p. 77.
58. Ibid, p. 78.
59. Johanna Eggert, Missionsschule und Sozialer Wandel in Ost-Afrika, Bertelsmann Universitätsverlag, Bd. 10, 1970, p. 150.
60. H. W. Schönmeier, op. cit., pp. 40-47.
61. Abdallah bin Hemedi Ajjemy, Habari za Wakilindi, EALB, 1972, pp. 35-39.
62. S. Feierman, op. cit., pp. 21-32.
63. L. Storch, Sitten, Gebräuche und Rechtspflege bei Bewohnern Usambaras, Berlin 1895, pp. 310-315.
64. S. Feierman, op. cit., pp. 28-35.
65. H. W. Schönmeier, op. cit., pp. 66-67.
66. L. Storch, op. cit., p. 322.
67. S. Feierman, op. cit., pp. 36-38.
69. GTZ (Deutsche Gesellschaft für Technische Zusammenarbeit), op. cit., p. 62.

IV. THE RESPONSE OF THE LOCAL PEASANTRY TO WAGE-LABOUR IN THE SISAL PLANTATIONS

Chapter Three examined the general characteristics of the Tanga Region, which included its location, size, physiography, climate, population structure and the social organisation of the local people. The examination was important for the reader's comprehension of the background of the research questions and other issues to be discussed in the study.
This Chapter will investigate the wage-labour question in the region with respect to the sisal plantations. The Tanga region is the centre of the sisal industry in Tanzania.

The need to undertake this investigation arises from the argument propagated that the rural areas in Tanzania are characterized by a surplus of labour which is underemployed, and that it would be advisable to engage this underemployed labour in productive activities such as wage labour in the sisal plantations.[1]
This hypothesis is based on lack of information concerning the living and working conditions in the sisal plantations. For instance, very few local people from the rural areas of the Tanga region, where most of the sisal plantations are located prefer to take wage labour in them. This is because the plantations do not offer them any social security; the wages are low and the working and living conditions are very poor.
Moreover, there has been contraversies and premature generalizations about the characteristics of the African working class. One way of avoiding this generalization is to examine the history and characteristics of different groups of workers at their particular place of employment.

We shall begin this investigation with a presentation and analysis of the different theories concerning the African working class and later see their application to the sisal plantations. These theories include those of orthodox Marxists and liberal scholars. The concept of 'social classes' and its application to the African conditions has already been examined in detail in Chapter Two (2.1) of this work.

4.1. Theories on African Wage-labour

We shall begin with the arguments of the scholars with an orthodox Marxist conception. These tend to see the evolution of the African working class as similar to that of the proletariat in the western capitalist societies. They argue that in many African countries the small producers in the rural areas have lost their rights in land through land alienation or overpopulation. Those who may be said to own their means of production, their ownership is just nominal because they are easily compelled to submit to exploitation by the ruling classes. They go on to argue that the African urban work force is much more stable and committed to paid employment than is commonly supposed. Furthermore, the need for economic development in the new states of Africa has deepened the development of capitalist relations: stimulating increased foreign investment, often in partnership with the indigenous state; and proletarianising the peasantry into a source of cheap labour for the capitalist employers.[2]

However, the Marxist theorists acknowledge that the forms of the above changes, as well as their rate, differ from area to area. But their main thesis remains that

the dominance of the capitalist mode of production in
the African economies is indisputable. They oppose the
ideology of African Socialism which gives a rosy picture
of the traditional African societies, especially the
function of the extended family as a redistributive
mechanism which reduces the veils of exploitation and
domination experienced in the capitalist system of western
countries. According to the Marxist scholars this ideology
serves the interests of the dominant classes in Africa.
It legitimates their monopoly of state power through
single-party regimes and appropriation of wealth through
the state.[3]

The opponents of the orthodox Marxist range from those
who see that it is still premature to apply a class
terminology to wage-earners or other social groups in
Africa because economic differentiation is not yet far
enough,[4] to those who maintain that because of his migrant character and ties to the land, the African worker
is so different from the proletariat in the industrialized
societies that comparisons are misleading and are not
possible. They argue that whereas the capitalist economic
structure in Europe developed out of feudal societies,
the level of socio-economic development in Africa has
not yet reached the conditions for the development of
capitalist production relations. They point out that
one necessary condition for the development of capitalist
relations of production is the existence of an 'army'
of wage labourers who own nothing except their labour
power. In Europe this 'army' was formed through the
separation of small-producers (peasants in the villages
and craftsmen in towns) from their means of production.
In tropical Africa where communal forms of land ownership
still exist, the African smallholder producer is ensured
of existence and is not forced by economic necessity

to go out of his village and sell his labour power to
the capitalist.[5]
Their conclusion is that 'true proletarians' with only
labour power to exchange are only just emerging in Africa
and this proletariat is a product of establishment of
colonial administration and European settlement.

However the liberal scholars accept that the appropriation
of labour power has been widespread in indigenous African
societies. Various forms of chattel and domestic slavery
was common and groups of workers like the Aro age groups
of Yorubaland, the Ankofone of Sierra Leone or the Ruga
Ruga of Western Tanzania, were engaged in house building
or heavy farming on contractual basis. Moreover, within
pre-colonial African towns, traditional crafts and guilds
were well-established, most of which involved the use
of apprentice.[6] For example, M. B. Akpan shows that
the Americo-Liberian settlers (who were ironically agricultural labourers in origin themselves) used apprentices
as cheap farm labour. In 1887 it was estimated that
every American-Liberian had 6 to 8 'apprentices' while
the President of the Republic alone had 120 youths in
service.[7]

Nevertheless, Michaela von Freyhold points out that
those who performed labour services for others during
the pre-colonial period never lost their right to a
livelihood from land and the tools of production belonging
to them. The labour services they offered were done
under fixed social obligations or on the basis of voluntary
consent between the parties concerned.[8]

Three main features of the African working class are
identified: (i) workers in Africa do not constitute
a permanent urbanised, proletarianized class. They are

an amorphos collection of migrant workers with rights
to land in rural areas, hence not fully separated from
their means of production and reduced to a level on
which they "have nothing to lose"; (ii) the urban workers
in Africa are not exploited. They are a highly-paid
aristocracy attuned to political conservatism by being
better off than the 'wretched of the earth' in the rural
areas; (iii) the inculcation of revolutionary consciousness in the African worker is a hopeless task, given
his commitment to ethnic consciousness and the maintenance
of his rural roots.[9]

The orthodox Marxists can be criticized for failing
to take note of the special features which differentiate
the development of the working class in underdeveloped
societies like those of Africa. A study made by the
United Nations International Labour Organisation (ILO)
in ten African countries (see Table 4.1) indicates that
wage earners in Africa constitute a small part of the
total and economically active population. A segment
of this class remains migrant or semi-proletarianised,
earning part of its living by production from land.
Furthermore the owners of capital in Africa have been
largely foreign, although state control is now in the
hands of the local administrators.[10] What is equally
important is that the labour movement in the African
societies have evolved within a different class context.
In the colonial period foreign and local conflicts (racial
conflicts, the nationalist movements etc.) were the major
issues for the working class struggles. In the post-
colonial era, however, varying patterns of relationships
betwen labour, the state and foreign capital are only
beginning to emerge. These considerations aim at suggest-
ing that capitalism in underdeveloped societies breeds
a distinctive proletariat within a distinctive peripheral
social context.

Table: 4.1

A COMPARISON BETWEEN WAGE-EARNERS IN 10 AFRICAN COUNTRIES AND 10 INDUSTRIALIZED COUNTRIES SURVEYED BY ILO IN 1982. (Total Population and Wage-Earners in Millions of People)

AFRICAN COUNTRIES

COUNTRY	(a)	(b)	(c)	(d)	I	II	III
BENIN	3.3	1.1	0.04	0.01	13.0	3.9	21
BOTSWANA	0.9	0.3	0.10	0.02	11.0	30.0	20
BURUNDI	4.2	1.9	0.04	0.01	1.0	2.2	27
CAMEROON	7.7	2.7	0.40	0.05	5.0	14.0	14
KENYA	17.0	8.0	1.04	0.19	6.1	13.0	18
MALAWI	6.0	2.4	0.32	0.11	5.4	13.5	34
NIGER	5.2	2.0	0.04	0.01	0.7	1.7	35
SWAZILAND	1.0	0.3	0.08	0.02	8.0	27.0	25
TANZANIA	20.0	9.6	0.80	0.12	3.8	7.8	16
ZAMBIA	7.0	2.1	0.38	0.03	5.4	18.0	8

INDUSTRIALIZED COUNTRIES

COUNTRY	(a)	(b)	(c)	(d)	I	II	III
DENMARK	5	3	3	1	51	87	40
FRANCE	54	24	21	8	39	89	39
HOLLAND	14	6	5	2	36	83	32
ITALY	57	23	21	7	36	89	33
JAPAN	119	58	56	22	48	98	39
NORWAY	3	2	2	1	63	95	42
SWEDEN	6	4	4	2	70	96	45
U.K.	56	26	23	10	41	88	41
U.S.A.	232	112	100	43	43	89	44
W.GERMANY	62	28	25	10	41	89	41

(a)=Total Population   (b)=Economically Active Population   (c)=Wage-Earners   (d)=Women Wage-Earners
I =(c)as percentage of(a)   II =(c)as percentage of(b)   III =(d)as percentage of(c)

ILO = United Nations International Labour Organisation

Source: ILO, Year Book of Labour Statistics, Geneva, 1983

Table 4.1 also indicates that compared to the advanced
capitalist societies, in African countries the participation of women in wage labour is still very small. This
is due to their low level of education compared to men
and certain traditional norms in the different African
tribes which limit the role of women to family, agricultural and domestic labour force.[11]

The liberal theorists on the other hand can be criticised
on the following points:
(i) they fail to understand the peculiar character of
class exploitation which exists in Africa, i.e. in most
countries in Africa one finds large numbers of peasants
and small commodity producers who may be said to own
their means of production like land, but this ownership
is just nominal, because they are easily compelled to
submit to exploitation. The classical pattern of capitalist exploitation whereby the private capitalist appropriates the difference between the value produced by
the worker's labour and the value of that labour, does
exist in Africa, but it is not necessarily the most
prevalent method of exploitation. In Africa much of
the exploitation is not done by individual capitalists,
but by the state acting as entrepreneur. All over Africa
the state has become a powerful entrepreneur, establishing business and hiring wage-labour.[12] As regards the
existing individual capitalists in African countries,
Szymon Chodak has the following to say:

> "The individual African entrepreneur can hardly be
> describes as a capitalist. Rarely does he venture
> to engage in large scale industrial activities em-
> ploying numerous workers ... African businessmen
> engage in retail trade, transportation, or small
> construction work ... They prefer to invest their
> money in a number of smaller enterprises bringing
> modest profits in a short time rather than in bigger
> ventures, the outcome of which is difficult to anti-
> cipate. They employ only a few employees and most
> often recruit for the job their distant relatives ...

> New and unexperienced in their undertakings, they
> had in the past to face the competition of long estab-
> lished European and Asian companies. If they succeed
> in this competition it was because of their private,
> individual good connection with the men in state
> power ... quite often they are actually relatives
> of the members of the political or bureaucratic elite
> and ... operate with money belonging to their power-
> ful patrons ..." 13

African societies appear to be classless because of
the wide prevalence of simple commodity production,
the rudimentary development of the forces of production
and the smallness of the urban proletariat.

(ii) one of the Marxist concepts which has sometimes
been misused is that of 'labour aristocracy'. V. I.
Lenin who popularised it never vigorously defined it
himself. In his writings he started with the notion
of labour aristocracy as a small minority of skilled
artisans and better paid workers, then applied it to
mean the permanent officialdom of reformist trade unions
and parties. He later extended its use to the entire
proletariat of the imperialist world, as allegedly benefiting from capitalist super-exploitation of the colonial
and ex-colonial world. This has made his concept politically and intellectually a suspect one.[14]

In respect to its application to Africa, the concept
of 'labour aristocracy' has been used to deny the utility
of class analysis; to justify policies holding down
the wage levels of African workers; to control their
organised expressions and attribute political conservatism
to them.[15] This point is supported by K. Hinchcliffe
who says that the application of the labour aristocracy
thesis in Africa is based on a comparison of rural and
urban incomes as evidence of class differences. It does
not take into consideration that the real living standards

of urban workers in Africa are not in the average significantly higher than those of the rural masses. The higher costs of living in the urban areas, transfer of income from urban workers to rural families and the greater insecurity of the worker compared to the peasant, have all been ignored by the advocators of this thesis.[16]

H. Gallis who has made a comprehensive study of the development of the working class in Africa before and after independence says:
> "... since independence, cities have grown and the number of people seeking jobs and living in urban centres has tripled. Yet, the number of those actually employed as workers, remains approximately the same as before ... Most of the people who call themselves workers ... are actually migrant labourers who still retain connections with their native areas. They return there either periodically or in time of crisis ..." 17

One of the major characteristics shown in the literature dealing with employment in the developing countries is extreme income differences between the different areas of employment, especially in the urban areas.[18] For instance in 1975 an ILO mission estimated that in the major towns of Kenya, there were about 350,000 employees, but only 3 % of these earned 300 Kenyan Pounds or more per annum. The rest of the urban work force earned 100 pounds or less per annum. The small group of highly paid workers were employed in the few foreign-owned industries like breweries and soft drinks, chemicals, oil and petrol, printing and cigarette-making (BAT). This implies that a stratum of better-off workers does exist in Africa, but to include all the wage-earners in the continent in the category of a 'labour aristocracy' would be unfair. Moreover, the presence of large numbers of job seekers in the urban areas creates a sense of insecurity among all sections of the employed workforce. Colin Leys adds that so long as the process of underdevelopment in Africa kept the rate of growth of employment opportunities below that of population growth, socio-economic insecurity for those employed and the job seekers becomes critical.[19]

My own position as far as this investigation of the theories on wage-labour in Africa is concerned, is that due to the low level of industrialization the working class in Africa is still a very small part of the total and economically active population. Moreover, as a result of low wages and socio-economic insecurity, especially in old age, most members of this class still maintain close ties with their rural origins. In his work on 'A Rural-Urban Network Model in Kenya', Thomas Weisner says:
> "... even highly-placed civil servants ... looked on some rural plot as 'home' ... four out of five wage-earners wanted to retire to the countryside ..." 20

The following sections will make a historical examination of the wage labour question in the sisal plantations of the Tanga region and see how the above discussed theories apply to it.

4.2. Introduction of the Sisal Industry and the Wage Labour Question in the Sisal Plantations

4.2.1. Introduction of the Sisal Industry

The beginning of the sisal industry in the Tanga region and to a great extent in Tanzania itself goes back to the time when the plant was introduced in the former German East Africa by a German agronomist, Dr. Richard Hindorf, who was employed by the German East African Company. He arrived in Tanga in 1891 after visiting the

Far East where he was looking for tropical plants which
could be grown in the German East African colony.
During his stay in Tanga he was concerned with finding
a plant suitable to the conditions of the plains from
the Usambara Mountains to the coast of Tanga where there
is moderate, but sufficient rainfall. Through his con-
tacts with a plant dealer in Florida, the Beasoner Bros.
Company, he managed to obtain the first sisal plants
which would form the foundation for the sisal industry
in Tanzania.
The Beasoner Brothers delivered one thousands bulbils
by way of Hamburg. However, only 62 plants reached Tanga
safely. Dr. Hindorf planted the bulbils at Kikongwe on
the southern side of the Pangani river in 1893.
In 1905 the "Westdeutsche Handels- u. Plantagengesell-
schaft" imported 1000 bulbils direct from Mexico. Apart
from these importations, the development of the industry
relied on the natural increase of the planted material.
By 1911 there were 54 sisal estates in the country,
eighty percent of which were in the Tanga region.[21]

4.2.2. Background to the Wage Labour Problem

One of the problems which faced the establishment and
development of the sisal industry was that of securing
enough labour power. In contries like Brasil, sisal
was introduced as a peasant crop in smallholdings. In
Tanzania, however, sisal has been a plantation crop
since its introduction.
Combining both field agriculture and a degree of first-
stage processing, the sisal plantations require large
amounts of land, capital and labour. Therefore, juxtaposed to the traditional economy in Tanzania where a
proletarian class did not exist, the institution of
the plantation system required the creation of conditions

for the emergence of free labour that was divorced from
the means of production.

The peasants around the plantations had no economic
necessity to look for wage employment. Moreover, some
of the local people were hunters, fishermen or cattle
herders and were not used to cultivation work. This fact
was not fully realized by the first European planters,
since they expected the peasants to flock to their plantations through the normal market mechanisms.[22]
The plantation owners also underestimated the level
of subsistance wages that would have attracted the peasants.
Imbued with racial prejudices, the planters discounted
the value of the security of subsistance which the traditional sector provided for the peasants. This security
included the peasant's daily means of subsistance and
the support he would receive from the community during
old age or sickness.

The wage income promised by the planters and their recruiting agents not only fell short of what the peasant
would need to support his family, but was unreliable
as well. In addition, the conditions of work in the
plantations were very unsatisfactory. Once employed
under contract, which was either written or more often
oral, the labourers were subjected to harsh conditions
for breaking the contract.
The institution of contract in an illiterate society,
where the employer had the monopoly over the ability
to read, write and speak the language of the law provided
sufficient opportunities for abuses which were intended
to keep the labourer in employment longer than he de-
sired.[23]
Besides the abuse of the contract, there was the brutality
of the planters and settlers. In 1907 the Secretary

of State and Director of the Colonial Office in Germany
inspected German East Africa and recorded the following
observations:

> "... nearly every whiteman walks around with a whip
> ... and almost every white man indulges in thrashing
> any blackman he wants. The legal basis of this is
> found in the law which permits an employer moderate
> corporal punishment of his servants ... The legal
> right to corporal punishment is also vested in the
> Managers of the Plantations and their assistants.
> The latter are partly immature youngsters, who, having
> just arrived, see themselves already as educators
> of the black race ..." 24

The living conditions of the labourers three decades
after the establishment of the sisal industry are described in an annual Medical Report as follows:

> "... On arrival at the plantations the labourers
> were turned on to build any sort of shelter and within
> a day or two were put to work. The diet issued was
> deficient in quality and variety. There was no ade-
> quate arrangement for latrines, water supply etc.
> As a consequence dysentry, bowel troubles and death
> ensued, and the proportion rendered unfit was large." 25

The hatred of the local people around the plantations
and the labourers against the Planters in Tanga is reflected in the words of the settler St. Paul Illeire:

> "... Daß die Mehrzahl unserer Eingeborenen mit unserer
> Herrschaft nicht zufrieden sind, darüber wollen wir
> uns keiner Täuschung hingeben ... Man fühlte sich
> immer wie auf einem Pulverfaß, das jeden Augenblick
> explodieren konnte ..." 26

Inspite of the above unfavourable conditions, the peasants
who refused to work on the plantations or who worked
only occasionally were regarded by the planters as irrat-
ional.

4.2.2.1. Colonial Efforts to Solve the Labour Problems

The divorce between the peasantry and their means of production has proceeded very slowly. Political coercion was the first means to drive the local people into the labour market. Robin Cohen states that forced labour was an accepted and widely practised part of the policies of the colonial powers, in order to 'persuade' Africans to accept the work ethic.[27] Sharon Stichter adds that state intervention into the labour market was necessary because the demand for labour greatly exceeded the voluntary supply.[28] The labour question in German East Africa and later under British rule became a central point in the economy. This was due to the following reasons: First, the rapid expansion of European plantations became a factor. Between 1910 and 1914 the area of cultivated land increased by 207 %, but the number of labourers increased by only 38.3 %.[29] Second, the plantations were concentrated in a small area of the country, i.e. in the Tanga region.
Since not enough voluntary labour could be found, the colonial authorities often resorted to forced recruitment.[30]

During the period of rule by Governor von Götzen there were two methods of getting labour power for the plantations, as well as for public projects such as building roads, railways, government houses etc.:
First, the allocation of labourers in the plantations was organised from the neighbouring areas. The District Officer ordered the 'Akidas' to organise this labour and the latter in turn directed the village chiefs to do this in their respective areas. For instance, in western Usambara each shamba peasant was issued with a labour card which required him to spend thirty days a year on

a European plantation. This was the 'Wilhelmstaler Arbeitskarten System'.[31]

Second, since 1895 labourers were imported from the inland provinces to work in plantations in the Tanga region and other coastal areas. The task of recruitment was handled by Goans, Arabs, Indians and some Europeans. These were paid on a per capita basis upon delivery, which led to bribery and deception in the transactions. The recruiting agents corrupted the village chiefs and Akidas with various presents in order to get more labourers and presented false information regarding the future employment.[32]

The use of force was also common in obtaining labourers. One District Officer reported the following:

"Ein Europäer drohte den Häuptlingen mit Prügel, wenn sie ihm keine Arbeiter beschafften ..." [33]

Forced labour, however, became unpopular with the colonial government when it was found to be one of the major causes of the 'Maji Maji' Uprising in 1905 to 1907.

In February 1909, Governor Rechenberg set out to curb the abuse on the plantations by passing a new labour legislation. The new ordinance covered labourers employed for more than one month and declared the following:
- labour recruits had to be given standard contracts and these contracts must be registered with a labour commissioner;
- the maximum period of contract permissible was to be either seven months or 180 working days out of nine months;
- employers had to provide food rations or regular payments for all days and for eight 'idle' days per month. The latter included sundays and holidays. The ration was to be equivalent to 1/3 of the total wage. They were also obliged to provide adequate housing, medical care and return transport to the villages after the contract;

- the working day was limited to 10 hours and workers
  were to be given adequate time to perform their private
  domestic chores by day light;
- employers lost the right to punish their workers.
  They had to apply to the district authorities to have
  their disobedient workers beaten or imprisoned by
  the state;
- breach of contract by either side became punishable
  offence.[34]

The settlers and planters were against this new labour
decree. They claimed that it worked more in the interests
of the natives than themselves. Therefore as a reaction
to the new ordinance they formed the 'Wirtschaftliche
Landesverband von Deutsch-Ostafrika' in Juni 1909. It
demanded the following measures from the colonial government:
- the expansion of the "Wilhelmstaler Labour Card System"
  to other parts of the region;
- labour control to reduce the break-up of contracts
  through journeys or Dismissal Passes for migrant labourers;
- establishment of a permanent labour recruiting Bureau.

The Governor refused all these requests for the fear
of native resistance. However, in practice, most of
the provisions of the new labour ordinance were difficult
to enforce since inspections of the plantations were
rare and the workers were hardly in a position to fight
for the rights they had been granted. Moreover, the
employers used one loophole of the legislation, namely
the absence of any regulation for casual labour employed
for one month or less, to their advantage.
Another measure taken to force the peasants to undertake
wage employment in European enterprises was the intro-

duction of taxation. In 1897 the German colonial administration issued a taxation ordinance, which was enacted also by the British in 1922. Areas under full political control were subjected to a hut tax whose main objective was to oblige the peasants to accept paid labour and accustom themselves to European administrative discipline.[35]
This mechanism failed to work satisfactorily because the taxation did not discriminate between incomes derived from the sale of labour power and the sale of agricultural products. Taxation also created a migratory type of labour particularly for the indigenous people around the plantations. Moreover, the hut tax had the social effect of reducing the number of huts built. This was predominantly the case in Handeni where many men escaped into the bushes, which led to the taxation of women who had to pay by forced labour.[36]

The British proceeded to regulate labour relations by passing a 'Master and Servant Ordinance' in 1923. The Ordinance had the following elements:
- recruiting of labourers was limited to licensed labour agents and contracts had to be testified by an administrative officer who ascertained that the labourer understood the implication of the contract;
- employers were again obliged to provide food, housing and medical care. The maximum period of time for the contract was extended to 2 years;
- desertion was a criminal offense punishable by a fine not exceeding Tsh. 100 and/or imprisonment for 6 months. A contract was not considered to be terminated by this punishment but had to be completed afterwards;
- employers on the other hand could be punished for breach of contract by a fine of Tsh. 200 and/or imprisonment for one month.

These regulations made contracts longer and sanctions
against breaking them heavier.
In 1926 a new Ordinance covering short-term contracts
of 30 to 60 working days was enacted. This was a piece-
work contract (Kipande) but was legally binding and
subject to fine and imprisonment.
The basic characteristics of these legislations remained
in force until independence, despite some amendments.[37]
Despite the attempts of regulation through various pieces
of legislation under German and British rule, actual
jurisdiction was in favour of the employer. In 1944,
for instance, 93 employers were prosecuted under the
'Master and Servant Ordinance' with 44 of them (47 %)
being convicted, i.e. 39 were fined and 5 were imprisoned.
Of the 147 employees who were prosecuted in the same
year, 114 (78 %) were convicted; i.e., 12 were fined,
9 received corporal punishment and 93 (63 %) were imprisoned.[38]
The major offence for which employers were prosecuted
was the poaching of labour, and their successful prose-
cution benefited only fellow capitalists and not the
labourers. Whereas labourers were mainly punished for
breach of contract or neglect in fulfilling their contracts.

The demand for cheap labour in the plantations during
the British rule was further met by pushing the Waha
people of Kigoma region into the labour market through
imposing heavy taxes on the peasants and preventing
them from growing cash crops. By the 1930s labourers
were imported from as far away as Ruanda and Burundi
and Mozambique. In 1944 the Tanganyika Sisal Growers
Association organised a 'Sisal Labour Bureau', commonly
known in Tanzania as 'SILABU'. Until 1965 this bureau
was responsible for recruiting labourers on contract

lasting 2 to 2 1/2 years.[39] It had its major operations in Lindi, Mtwara, Ruvuma and Kigoma regions.[40]

Although SILABU did not resort to either force or fraud, it remained unpopular with most workers until it was abolished, since it was engaged in the marketing of human beings. It reminded the people of the time of slave trade. Moreover, each recruited labourer from upcountry was given a number, and as a result of these numbers they were known among the local people of Tanga region as 'MANAMBA'.[41]

The poor working conditions in the plantations led the local people to seek temporary jobs while maintaining the security afforded by their membership in their kinship group. The failure of the sisal plantation system to proletarianize the peasantry in the region had the following long lasting effects:

(i) the migrant nature of the labourers led to the perpetuation of the unskilled character of the labour force in the region and the country at large;

(ii) it became evident that the major cause of absenteeism, lack of initiative and productivity of the sisal labourers was due to the character of the plantation system itself rather than the traditional society of the labourers;

(iii) the system of migrant labour, especially for the labourers who were recruited from outside the region, impeded innovation and development in their traditional societies. This created a vicious circle in which poverty caused migration and migration in turn hindered the elimination of poverty.

The sisal industry remined the main source of employment in Tanzania until the early 1960 as shown in Table 4.2. In 1963 it represented 35.9 % of the total employment in the country. Since 1964, however, the sisal industry has experienced a fall in demand on the world market due to competition with synthetic fibres and other sisal producers like Brazil.[42]

Table 4.2: <u>Percentages of the Contribution of the Sisal Industry to Total Employment in the Economy of Tanzania</u>

Year	% of Total Employment
1961	37.3
1962	38.3
1963	35.9
1964	33.6
1965	27.9
1966	22.9
1971	9.0
1972	9.1
1973	8.7
1974	8.7
1978	8.0
1980	6.8

Source: Bureau of Statistics, <u>Employment and Earning Survey</u>, DSM 1981, p. 31

4.3. The Nationalization Policy and Characteristics of Wage Labour in the Present Sisal Plantation System

The past sections examined the background of the labour problem in the sisal plantations during the colonial period until the beginning of the decline of the position of the sisal industry in the Tanzania's economy in the 1960s. This section will carry further this investigation after the nationalization policy of 1967.

4.3.1. The Nationalization Policy

In October 1967, the government nationalized fully or partly over 60 % of the major sisal estates in the country as part of the Arusha Declaration to bring the major means of production under state control. Six sisal companies registered outside the country were totally nationalised. The largest of these were: the British-owned Bird and Company Ltd., which had 12 estates; the Dutch N. V. Cultur Matschappij with 4 plantations; the Kulasi Plantation; the Kilimajaro Sisal Plantation and the Niko Plantation.[43] The estates owned by these six nationalised companies formed the core of the Tanzania Sisal Corporation, which later became the current Tanzania Sisal Authority (TSA). The Corporation has the following objective:

> "to conduct the business of the sisal growers, processors, exporters, manufacturers of the sisal product ..." [44]

Thirty three other sisal companies registered in Tanzania were partly nationalized, with the government holding the majority of the shares. Moreover, all nationalized or partly nationalized plantations were fully compensated.[45]

4.3.2. Characteristics of Wage-Labour in the Present Sisal Plantation System

4.3.2.1. Categories of Employees

The labour force in the present sisal plantations of the Tanga region consists of three main categories of employees: the 'permanent workers', the casual labourers, and the so-called 'contractor's labourers'.[46] The employees on 'permanent' basis are registered on each estate's Master-rolls.[47] The conditions of their contract generally approximate those laid down by the law. The workers are warned before or served with notices concerning termination of their employment. They are often properly paid their due wages according to the minimum wage law, with appropriate fringe benefits such as leave, the National Provident Fund[48] etc. Fees for their membership to the National Labour Union (JUWATA) are often deduced from wages and paid by the employer.

However the term 'permanent' employees, by which the workers in this category are generally referred to is misleading. The nature of employment fluctuations in the plantation as shown in table 4.3 is such that permanency is almost non-existent.

Table 4.3: <u>Total Average Labour Force</u>[a] <u>per Annum in Tanzania Sisal Plantation System 1960-1980</u>

Year	No. of Persons in the Labour Force
1960	109,809
1965	63.066
1970	26,633
1975	32,540
1980	54,400

(a) = Workers registered in the Master-rolls

<u>Source</u>: TSA, <u>Labour Force Annual Reports</u>, Tanga

Table 4.3 shows also that between 1960 and 1970 nearly 83,176 employees lost their employment. Therefore extreme insecurity of losing one's livelihood due to frequent unemployment is one of the characteristics of the employment in the present sisal plantation system. Demand for labour force depends on the world market situation of the sisal product.[49] Moreover, the wages in the plantations are still very low compared to the present minimum wage in government employment (Tsh. 600 per month). In 1950 the wages for the so-called 'permanent employees' in the plantations were between Tsh. 38 and Tsh. 54 per month. By 1960 they had increased to between Tsh. 84 and Tsh. 111 including rations of food valued at Tsh. 21. By the time of this field study in February 1983, the minimum wage for the permanent workers had risen to Tsh. 450 per month.

In theory casual labourers are covered by law. Their terms of service and minimum wage are defined by law, but these terms are not adhered to by the plantation management. For instance the estates monthly and annual reports are expected to indicate the total number of employees of this category as in others, but in practice, this is not the case.
Labour statistics in the sisal industry was started by the colonial planters as a method of deciding on the recruitment and distribution of labour during the colonial period when recruitment was a centralized undertaking in the industry. The termination of this approach in 1965 put an end to labour statistical precision in the sisal industry in Tanzania. It is not uncommon today to find an estate recording the number of casual labourers as say "20" each month throughout the year, just as a formality.[50]

The 'contractor's labour' is the least privileged worker category. The term is derived from the arrangement made between the plantation management and a private labour employer. The employer contracts with the sisal plantation management to complete a certain piece of work for a certain sum of money. He then recruits labourers from the local settlements alongside plantations, known commonly by the local people as 'Mwisho wa shamba' or elsewhere in the plantation region. They are paid per piece of work completed. They have virtually no other contract terms and are paid not much more than half the normal wage. In this case the employer is the labour contractor and not the management of the plantation. S. Kajumba argues that these private employers should in fact be called "Labour racketeers" because they obtain their incomes through trading in human labour power.[51]

The number of labourers in all the three categories is subject to manipulation by the employers for necessary adjustments of labour costs at appropriate moments. This makes labour figures in the plantations unreliable.

4.3.2.2. Sex Structure

C. W. Guillebaud observed that in the Java sisal industry, women constituted the significant category of labour force in that they were the cutters of the sisal leaves.[52] In the sisal industry of Tanzania, however, it would be unthinkable for a woman to cut sisal. For instance in 1980 women constituted 9 % of the labour force in the plantations but none of them was involved in the cutting of sisal leaves.[53] Most of the women are concentrated in the light jobs such as sisal nurseries, weeding and carrying the dry sisal fibre from the drying lines into the 'brushrooms'.

4.3.2.3. Age and Education

In terms of the age of 'permanent workers' the range was according to our findings from 18 to 68 years, with an average of 32 years.
An average of 56 % of the workers registered in the Masterrolls of the plantations visited during the field study were aged between 25 and 43 years. One implication about the general pattern of age in the sisal plantations is that sisal workers seem to retire voluntarily soon after the age of 43. This is because the plantations do not offer old age socio-economic security. Therefore, it is prudent for the workers to return to their villages of origin before they are too old.
A study made by Ndawula Kajumba also showed that only 10 % of the permanent workers in the sisal plantations of the Tanga region were above 40 years of age.[54]

As regards the level of education of the 'permanent workers' the standard was observed to be very low. Only 30 % of th randomly selected workers in the estates visited could at least read and write in Kiswahili, although more than 50 % of them claimed to have attended school up to four years.
Very few jobs on the sisal estates require formal education.[55]

4.3.2.4. Tribal Origin of the Workers

The purpose of this part is to show that it does not necessarily follow that spatial proximity to the plantations is associated with a tendency to work on them. Table 4.4 shows the distribution of the workers in the nine surveyed plantations in the Korogwe and Handeni Districts according to their place of origin, i.e. from tribal groups outside the region or local tribes (Shambaa, Zigua, Digo, Bondei and Segeju).

Table 4.4: <u>Origin of the Sisal Workers in 9 Surveyed Plantations in Korogwe and Handeni Districts</u>

Workers Origin	1980	1981	1982	Febr. 1983
Number of Workers from outside the region	721	832	873	2,480
Number of workers from local tribes	262	302	245	350
Total number of workers	983	1,134	1,118	1,830
Outsiders as % of Total	73.3	73.4	78.1	80.9

<u>Source:</u> Workers' Master Rolls and Work-Cards at Mazinde, Mabogo, Toronto, Ngombezi, Kwamdulu, Kwamndolwa, Mwelya, Kwamgwe, Kwaraguru Sisal Estates

In the period from 1980 to February 1983 an average of 76.4 % of the total number of workers in the surveyed plantations came from tribal groups outside the region. Most of these workers came into the region during the time of the Sisal Labour Bureau, i.e. 1944-1965. After the decline of the sisal industry which led to loss of employment, they settled in the neighbouring villages around the plantations working as casual labourers in the farms of the local people, when they failed to get pieces of land for their own cultivation. This is the case in the Korogwe district where most of the best land is occupied by sisal plantations.[56] The costs in terms of fare and material

expectactions by relatives in their villages of origin
prevented the unemployed labourers to return to their home
regions.[57]

In 1975, O.F. Lameck made a study on job duration by the
tribal categories of the workers in 6 sisal plantations
of the Tanga region (2 in Tanga district, 2 in Korogwe,
and 2 in Muheza). Table 4.5 gives the results of his study.
Table 4.5 shows that only two tribes, the Zigua and Shambaa, out of about five indigenous tribal groups in the
region were among the seven relatively represented groups
in the sample. The rest came from regions further from
the plantation areas. Most of the Makonde and all the Rundi
people come from outside Tanzania. The Makonde are originally from Mozambique and the Rundi from Rwanda.
The Makonde followed by the Rundi and the Yao (from Lindi
region) seem to be the most stabilized tribal groups in
the sisal labour force.

The most migratory of the seven groups listed on Table
4.5 are the Bena followed by the Ha people. Both of them
have their origin outside the Tanga region.
Only 6 of the Zigua had held their current jobs for 5 years
or less. The rest of the Zigua and Shambaa people had held
their jobs for 11 years and over. Most of them are concentrated in jobs like drivers, extension services and other
auxiliary activities. This suggests that while the local
people do not generally work in the plantations, the few
who do tend to stay for a relatively long time.

Table 4.5: <u>Duration of Current Job by Tribal Categories of the Workers in six Sisal Plantations of the Tanga Region (1975)</u>

Main Tribal Group	No. below 5 years	No. 6-10 years	No. 11 years and over
Makonde (a)	1	1	25
Rundi (a)	1	5	7
Ha (b)	10	-	10
Bena (b)	7	1	2
Yao (b)	2	3	4
Zigua (c)	6	-	14
Shambaa (c)	-	-	14
Others	23	9	62
Total	50	19	138

(a) = Non-Tanzanians
(b) = Tanzanians from outside the Tanga Region
(c) = Locals

Source: O.F. Lameck, <u>Trends and Forces in the Sisal Industry of Tanzania</u>, University of Dar es salaam 1975, p. 14.

Table 4.6 shows the distribution of the workers in the different activities of the nine sisal plantations surveyed during the field study in the Korogwe and Handeni districts according to their place of origin.
In the period between 1980 and February 1983 an average of more than 90 % of the total number of sisal cutters and in the decortication section came from tribal groups

outside the region. According to the interview with the
workers, the two sections of plantation work are the most
difficult ones. Most of the local people avoid these activities and are concentrated on jobs such as weeding,
transport, transplanting and other auxiliary jobs.

Interviews with the workers in the nine sisal plantations
visited during the field study gave the following reasons
for the refusal of the indigenous people of the region
to work permanently in the estates:

(i) the nature of the working conditions in the plantations
has not yet been much improved since the colonial
period. Given the low level of the technology of the
instruments of labour such as hoes, bush-knives etc.,
sisal work is still a very hard job. Moreover, the
plantations are covered by thorny bushes which are
infested with snakes and dangerous insects. According
to the TSA Planning Officer in Tanga, the TSA has
not enough funds to clean the estates, especially
given the present economic crisis facing the country.
The poor conditions of the estates make the work of
sisal cutters difficult and dangerous.
For instance in 1976 to 1978, the Tanzanian Sisal
Authority launched campaigns in various parts of the
country to recruit sisal cutters for its various plantations. The number of labourers which was required
to meet the immediate demands of its plantations was
five thousand people, but the Authority managed to
get only three thousand people. In two months time
it was reported that only less than ten percent of
those obtained were still working. The rest had run
away because of the poor working conditions.[58]

(ii) As already pointed out in section 4.3.2.1. of this
Chapter, the salaries in the plantations were extreme-

ly low especially taking into consideration of the
present economic crisis facing the country and the
great shortage of most necessary commodities like
soap, maize flour, clothes etc. These commodities
can only be obtained on the black market at very high
prices. For example, a bag of maize (90 kilogrammes)
costs up to Tsh. 1200/= on the black market. The wages
obtained by the labourers cannot cover these costs.
Therefore, most of the local peasants prefer to concentrate on the cultivation of subsistence crops such
as maize and others which could be sold on the black
market at high prices, rather than take permanent
employment in the sisal plantations.[59]

The refusal of the local peasants in the region to take
permanent wage-labour in the plantations imply that even
after independence and the nationalization of the sisal
plantations, the latter have failed to bring about the
proletarianization of the peasants in the Tanga region. This
conclusion is supported by Fuggles-Cochman, who points
out that the failure of the sisal plantation system in
Tanzania to attract more permanent labour has led to the
substitution of capital for labour. The consequence of
the latter is a fall in the number of men employed per
ton of output. Moreover, it perpetuates the unskilled labour
character in the plantations.[60]

According to the Senior Economist of the Tanzania Sisal
Authority at the Headquarters in Tanga, there is no definite programme until the time of this study to improve
the labour problem facing the sisal plantations. The forced
labour conditions which existed during the colonial period
and the recruitment through agencies like the Sisal Labour
Bureau cannot be applied now.

Table 4.6: Distribution of the Workers in Different Activities of the Sisal Plantations Surveyed in Korogwe and Handeni Districts (According to their Place of Origin)

Year	CUTTING				DECORTICATION				WEEDING				AUXILIARY		
Origin of Workers	1980	1981	1982	Feb. 1983	1980	1981	1982	Feb. 1983	1980	1981	1982	Feb. 1983	1980	1981	1982
Non-Tanga Region Tribes	349	404	446	555	123	142	163	265	88	110	107	287	161	176	157
Local People	32	40	21	32	12	15	15	25	119	136	100	123	99	111	109
Total No. of Workers	381	444	467	587	135	157	178	290	207	246	207	410	260	287	266
Non-Tanga Tribes as % of Total	91.6	91.0	95.5	94.5	91.1	90.4	91.6	91.4	42.5	44.7	51.7	70.0	61.9	61.3	59.0

Source: Workers' Master-Rolls / Work-Cards at Mazinde, Mabogo, Toronto, Ngombezi, Kwamnduli, Kwamndobwa, Mwelya, Kwamgure, Kuravaguru Sisal Estates.

Private sisal plantation companies like the Amboni Group
has tried to utilize the present shortage of essential
commodities in the country to attract labourers to its
plantations. Since 1982 it has started a programme (which
is also announced in Radio Tanzania) called in Kiswahili
'MKATO BORA', i.e. best sisal cutters. The labourers are
paid according to the amount of bundles of sisal leaves
they have cut during the month. For instance:

A piece of work of 110 bundles has a payment of Tsh. 700/=
" " 120 " " " " " 770/=
" " 130 " " " " " 850/=
" " 140 " " " " " 940/=
" " 150 " " " " " 1040/=

In order to make the labourer remain at the plantation
for a long time the wages are paid as follows:
At the first saturday of the month the labourer gets
Tsh. 100/=. At the 15th date of the month he gets Tsh. 220/=
and at the third saturday he gets Tsh. 100/=. The rest
of the salary is paid to him at the end of the month.
In addition the labourer is provided with a kilogramme
of sugar and a toilet soap free of charge at the 15th date
of the month. At the end of the month he gets a kilogramme
of sugar and a bar of washing soap. The rest of the subsistence requirements can be bought at the estate shop
on credit to be paid at the end of the month.

However, the programme has also been able to attract a
migrant type of labour and most of the labourers have come
to realise that the system is meant to tie them to the
plantation rather than help them economically. Moreover,
the system of buying commodities on credit from the estate
shop has put many workers on debts. This is because the
things they need are usually more than the amount of money
they earn at the plantation.[61]

Although it could be suggested that the state and privately owned sisal plantations should cooperate to find ways of improving the working and living conditions of the labourers, the sisal industry like the rest of the economy in Tanzania is so dependent on the world market that, the long term solution for its present problems would largely depend on changes in the external and internal forces which affect the economy as a whole. Nevertheless, it would be advisable to reduce the existing area of the plantations, especially those of the Tanzania Sisal Authority, which depend on the government financially, to match the available management and financial capacity. Moreover, given the low demand for sisal and its products on the world market, and the current food problems facing Tanzania, diversification of production from sisal to food crops could be introduced.

4.3.2.5. Workers' Ownership and Participation in Management

In a plantation system of production, ownership may be by private individual capitalists, companies or the state. Ownership by workers themselves is usually very limited. P. R. Lawrence shows that African smallholder participation in the production of sisal has so far been restricted to the growth of hedge sisal in both Tanzania and Kenya. Their share on the total production is very small. In 1960, for instance, it reached a maximum of 6 % of the total production in Tanzania but in 1977 as a result of rising quality requirements it dropped to 0,6 %.[62] After the nationalization policy of 1967 which put nearly 60 % of the sisal plantations under state control, the number of sisal estates owned by the workers themselves in various forms of cooperatives is not more than ten. The rest are properties of individuals or companies.[63] This alienation of labour from the ownership of the means of production in the plan-

tation system implies that the workers have no control
over decision-making processes. Their wages and terms of
services, reduction or expansion of production area are
decisions taken by the employer.

Even in the state owned sisal plantations the organs which
were supposed to help the workers to participate in the
management of their places of employment have experienced
a number of limitations: the workers' committees established
after the reorganisation of the trade union movement in
Tanzania were supposed to be the workers' consultative
organs on matters concerning their welfare at the enterprise level. But studies made on these committees have
shown that they are just instruments of the managements
to control the workers. Their main emphasis has always
been 'discipline'.
For instance 'JENGA' (the Magazine of the National Development Corporation) reported the following statement from
the Annual Conference of Managers:
> "The workers' Committee deals mainly with discipline.
> It does not deal with politics or personnel policy or
> even with other aspects of managements ..." 64

Moreover, ever since the National Union of Tanzania Workers (NUTA)[65] acquired its parastatal status in 1964, its
leaders being nominated by the government and getting its
funds by compulsory deductions from workers' wages, it has
ceased to be the tool of expressing workers' interests.
It has assumed the role of demobilising the workers by
warning them against 'disobedience'.[66]

The same applies to the 'workers' councils' established
after the Presidential Circular of 1970 with the purpose
of bringing the workers closer to the management and giving
them more say in the formulation of policies.[67] During
the opening of one of the councils in Dar es salaam the

Secretary General of the National Union of the Tanzania
Workers said the following:
> "... the workers' council must strive to promote and
> maintain harmony between the workers and the management;
> they are not gangs of trouble makers aimed at inter-
> fering and disrupting the duties of management ..." 68

The above statement implies that the leadership of the
National Union of Tanzania Workers assumes that the interests of the management and those of the workers are
always the same. As a result of this assumption, when the
workers' councils were established the managers of the
enterprises were made the chairmen of the councils; and
the heads of the enterprise sections became permanent members of the councils. The secretary of the council was
to be appointed by the management.

It is difficult to envisage how the workers' councils could
effectively influence the behaviour of the management if
the latter is given such leading roles in the workers'
councils. Moreover, the management consists of the usual
capitalist 'boards of directors' which has no workers'
representation.[69] Furthermore, the thesis on the harmony
between workers and management in Tanzania stems from the
fact that Tanzania's 'Ujamaa' socialist strategy does not
emanate from a dialectical class analysis of society. It
is just an "attitude of mind", and therefore has no clear
definition of a 'working class'. The Arusha Declaration
just envisages a socialist society in Tanzania in which
"all the people are workers".[70]

As a result of the absence of a clear class ideological
position, there has also been no conception of bureaucracy
as a structural phenomenon in society with its own interests
to perpetuate. Hence very few efforts have been done to
curb the development of the strength of the bureaucracy

in the country. This is mainly due to the ambiguous role
of the Party in the enterprises.

After the proclamation of the Arusha Declaration in 1967
the Party opened its branches vigorously in all places
of employment. Their main function was to explain and
interpret the policy of socialism and self-reliance to
the workers and managers. But in practice, the Party branches are not allowed to disuss aspects like planning, production, sales etc. Similarly, they cannot discuss workers'
grievances authoritatively. This is said to be the function
of the workers' committees. Yet these are the concrete
forms in which the party policy of socialism and self-
reliance can be explained and interpreted.
The Party Guidelines of 1972 state:
> "... The duty of a socialist party is to guide all activ-
> ities of the people. The government, parastatals,
> national institutions, etc. are instruments for imple-
> menting the party's policies ..." 71

Various studies have shown that the Party in Tanzania has
consistently found it difficult to act as a cohesive, strong
organising body. The radical pronouncements like the one
above, have mostly been a result of the ideological orient-
ations of individuals within the Party leadership rather
than of its organisational strength. At the grass-roots
level the activities of the Party also depend solely on
the qualities of isolated individuals. The party membership
is so amorphous that one cannot differentiate by any qualit-
ative standard a member from a non-member.[72] This lack
of organisational strength together with the low level
of education of the party leadership compared to the management, makes it difficult for the Party to play its
leading role in the national institutions in the interests
of the workers.

Therefore, we would like to suggest that, just as the
nationalizations were made with the 'conception' of reorganisation of the whole society in the interests of the
direct producers, i.e. workers and peasants, the conception of workers' participation in the management of
their places of employment should be taken seriously as
part of the new relations of production. This can only
be done when the Party has a clear class conception of
the 'working class'. This will help to improve th quality
of Party membership and differentiate the interests of
the workers and those of the management. This is supported
by Arnold Temu who says that despite the nationalizations,
the attitudes and management methods of those who have
been appointed to the run the nationalized institutions,
even though they are Tanzanians continue to be the same
as those of the colonial manager. This includes their relationship with the workers.[73]

There is also a need to have a well informed Party leadership at the enterprise level in order to strengthen its
influence over the management. This can be done through
encouraging the workers to improve their education con-
stantly.

Despite the above limitations of workers' participation
in the management of their places of employment, workers
in the sisal plantations and other areas of employment
in Tanzania, have since the colonial period struggled in
different forms against the oppression of the employers
and for better conditions of work. Sharon Stichter points
out that one of the most important neglected aspects of
early labour history in Africa is the extent to which even
a migrant and semi-proletarianised work force is capable
of individual and collective labour action.[74]
At the beginning of the establishment of the colonial

rule, the indigenous people in Tanzania struggled against being recruited as labourers for European and government enterprises. The Zigua people of Handeni joined the Arabs and Swahili people along the coast in the anti-colonial resistances. The same applies to the 'Maji Maji' Uprising of 1905 to 1907 against forced labour and cultivation of cotton in eastern and southern Tanzania. Some of those recruited by force to work in the plantations, fled away after being sent to the plantation areas. Those who were employed struggled for better conditions of work. As employers suceeded in lowering the real wages of the labourers, the latter retaliated by lowering their output.[75] Until 1926 the only government agency which was concerned with strikes was the police. The formation of trade unions and the right to strike was considered by the colonial authorities as illegitimate and unafrican.

Therefore, there were four main ways in which the workers without a trade union organisation could express their grievances to the employers:
(i) Personal approaches and petitions, i.e. individuals or small groups of labourers could approach the employers to present their problems concerning the working conditions. Individuals presenting such petitions had to be extremely humble to the employer, especially in the sisal plantations where access to the manager was almost impossible.
(ii) Council of elders. This was a colonial method of divide and rule. The employer picked up 'elders' from among the labourer of different milieux. These formed an informal organ of communication between the employer and the workers.
(iii) Desertion and Evasion of contract. As a result of the unbearable conditions of work, workers were forced to desert.

(iv) Strikes and riots. The Great Economic Depression which affected the world in the 1930s, brought with it a fall in the prices of all primary products including sisal. Wages were drastically reduced. Workers on a number of plantations stages strikes and riots. The leaders of the strikes were arrested and imprisoned.[76] In the years that followed the workers struggled through stoppages. In 1939, for instance, 22 stoppages were reported to the labour officer of the Tanga Province.[77]

Confronted with the repressive attitudes of the government, the individual unions which tried to struggle for the rights of the workers had no chance of survival. The workers needed a central union which could combine different work-enterprises. Given their low level of education and their migrant character, the workers were incapable of accomplishing this goal.

The institution which was eventually created to fulfil this function was dominated by members of the petty bourgeoisie. The latter were inspired by the example of a national trade union in neighbouring Kenya and the founding of the nationalist Party (Tanganyika African National Union) in 1954. They gathered the few existing unions and associations which were allowed by the colonial government to form the Tanganyika Federation of Labour in 1955. These associations include the African Commercial Employees Association, the Tanganyika Government Servants Association, and the Tanganyika Railways African Association. Their common characteristics was the high proportion of white collar workers among their members. There was no union for the sisal workers.
The Tanganyika Federation of Labour (TFL) existed until 1964, when it was replaced by the National Union of Tanzania

Workers. As already mentioned above the new organisation
is a parastatal, whose leadership is appointed by the government. Its weaknesses and those of the other organs
established to promote the interests of the workers,
especially after the nationalization policy have also been
discussed.

4.3.2.6. **Summary**

The purpose of Chapter Four was to make a historical and
empirical investigation of the response of the local peasantry in the Tanga region to wage labour in the sisal
plantations and the characteristics of the wage-labour
in the present sisal plantation system.

This investigation started with a presentation of the
different theories (from both scholars with an orthodox
Marxist persuation and liberals) concerning the nature
of the African working class. While the former theorists
see the development of the working class in Africa as
similar to that of the proletariat in western countries,
their opponents are divided between those who see that
it is still premature to apply a class terminology to the
social groups in Africa, because of the low level of economic differentiation, and the others argue that true proletarians with only labour power to exchange are only emerging in Africa. The Marxists were criticised for failing
to take note of the special features which differentiate
the development of the working class in Africa from those
of the advanced capitalist countries. The liberals on the
other hand fail to understand the peculiar type of exploitation of the small commodity producers whereby exploitation
is not done by individuals but by the state.

An examination of the historical development of the sisal
industry since the colonial period and the characteristics
of wage-labour in the present sisal plantation system
especially after the nationalization policy, has shown
that the sisal plantation system has failed to bring about
the proletarianization of the local peasantry in the region.
This is because of the poor working and living conditions.
The wages are low and the plantations do not offer any
social and economic security for the labourers. They have
managed to attract only a migrant type of labour. The effect
of which is the perpetuation of the unskilled labour character in the plantations.

An analysis of the workers' participation in management
has shown that the organs like workers' committees and
councils established to help the workers achieve the goal,
have been used by the management to control the workers.
The National Union of Tanzania Workers (which is controlled
by the government) has also dissociated with the interests
of the workers. It has assumed the role of warning them
against 'disobedience'.

Furthermore, the whole investigation of the question of
wage-labour in the sisal plantations has shown that it
is not justifiable to generalize the concept of labour
aristocracy to all the wage-earners in Africa. The working
and living conditions of the workers in the sisal plantations
of the Tanga region have shown that they are not better-
off than the peasantry in the rural areas. In fact most
of the workers maintain their relations with their rural
areas of origin because of the insecurity of employment
in the plantations.

In addition, the notion of political conservatism attributed
to the workers in Africa is also not justifiable. This

study has shown that despite of the limitations of workers'
participation in the management of their places of employment, workers in the sisal plantations and other areas
of employment in Tanzania have since the colonial period
struggled in different forms against the oppression of
the employers and for better conditions of work.

However, as a result of the low level of education and
their migrant character workers in the sisal plantations
were not able to form a trade union of their own.

Footnotes for Chapter Four

1. See C.W. Guillebaud, An Economic Survey of the Sisal Industry in Tanzania, TSGA, London 1966. Also F. Hitchcock, Notes on the Sisal Industry, Tanga, No. 2, 1967.

2. C. Ake, Explanatory Notes on Political Economy of Africa, in Journal of Modern African Studies, 14, 1(1976). Also see Essays collected in Richard Sandbrook and Robin Cohen (eds.), The Development of an African Working Class, Longman, London 1975.

3. The discussion of the process of peasant proletarianization in Africa was initiated by Giovanni Arrighi, Labour Supplies in Historical Perspectives: A Study of the Proletarianization of the African Peasantry in Rhodesia, The Journal of Development Studies, 3(1970). J.K. Nyerere's view of traditional Tanzania society has been challenged by non-Marxist Tanzanians like S.S. Mushi in Ujamaa: Modernisation by Traditionalisation, Taamuli, 1, 2(1971). Other critiques of African socialism include J. Mohan, Varieties of African Socialism, The Socialist Register, Monthly Review Press, Ne York 1966, and Ehud Sprinzak, African Traditional Socialism, in Journal of Modern African Studies, 2, 4(1973), pp. 629-47.

4. P. C. Lloyd, The New Elite of Tropical Africa, Oxford University Press 1966, p. 56, and J. C. Mitchell, Occupational Prestige and Social Status, Africa, 29(1959) pp. 35-6.

5. W. Elkan, Migrants and Proletarians, Oxford University Press 1960, in G. Arrighi and J. Saul, Nationalism and Revolutions in Sub-Saharan Africa, The Socialist Register. G. Arrighi, International Corporations, Labour Aristocracies and Economic Development in Tropical Africa, in R. I. Rhodes (ed.), Imperialism and Underdevelopment, Monthly Review Press 1970, pp. 234-5.

6. Richard Sandbrook, op. cit., p. 13.

7. M. B. Akpan, the African Policy of the Liberian Settlers, 1841-1930. A Study in the Native Policy of a Non-Colonial Power in Africa, Ph.D. Thesis, Ibadan 1968, pp. 158-9.

8. Michaela von Freyhold, The Formation of the Class of Wage-Labourers in Tanzania under Colonial Capitalism (Mimeo), DSM 1975, p. 9.

9. F. Fanon, The Wretched of the Earth, Penguin Books 1974.

10. C. Leys, Underdevelopment in Kenya, London 1975, pp. 118-19.

11. C. D. Deera, Rural Women's Subsistence Production in the Capitalist Periphery Economies, New York 1975, p. 83.

12. C. Ake, op. cit., p. 124.

13. S. Chodak, Social Stratification in Sub-Saharan Africa, Canadien Journal of African Studies, Vol. 7(1973), p. 414.

14. V. I. Lenin, Selected Works, Progress Publishers, Moscow 1972, pp. 68, 272, 604-6.

15. G. Arrighi and J. Saul, Essays on the Political Economy of Africa, Monthly Review Press, N. Y. 1973.

16. K. Hinchcliffe, Labour Aristocracy, A Northern Nigerian Case Study, in Journal of Modern African Studies, 12, 1(1974), pp. 57-68.

17. H. Gallis, The Size and Characteristics of Wage Employment in Africa, International Labour Review, Vol. 112, 3(1972).

18. E. Gerken, Arbeitsmärkte in Entwicklungsländern, Tübingen 191; also see C. Leys, op. cit., p. 180.

19. C. Leys, op. cit., p. 179.

20. T. S. Weisner, One Family, Two Households: A Rural-Urban Network Model of Urbanism, University of Nairobi (mimeo), 1978, p. 33.

21. A. C. Mascarenhas, Resistance and Change in the Sisal Plantation System of Tanzania, University of California, Los Angeles, Ph.D. Thesis (Unpublished), 1970, pp. 55-58.

22. J. Rweyemamu, Underdevelopment and Industrialization in Tanzania, A Study of Perverse Capitalist Development, Oxford University Press 1973, p. 17.

23. Michaela von Freyhold, op. cit., p. 15.

24. RKA, Nr. 300, Bl. 36.

25. Tanganyika Territory, Annual Medical Report, DSM, Government Printer 1924.

26. RKA, Nr. 300, Bl. 36.

27. Robin Cohen, Workers and Progressive Change in Underdeveloped Countries, London 1975, p. 13.

28. Sharon Stichter, The Formation of a Working Class in Kenya, in Richard Sandbrook (ed.), op. cit., p. 21.

29. O. T. Raum, German East Africa: Changes in African Life under German Administration, 1892-1914, in V. Harlow and E. M. Chilvers, History of East Africa, Vol. III, Oxford University Press 1965, p. 190.

30. Ibid., p. 184.

31. Michaela von Freyhold, op. cit., p. 7.

32. R. A. Austen, op. cit., p. 74.

33. RKA, Nr. 2o, Bl. 22.

34. Michaela von Freyhold, op. cit., p. 10.

35. J. Illife, Tanganyika Under German Rule, p. 160.

36. Michaela von Freyhold. Ujamaa Villages in Tanzania, An Analysis of a Social Experiment, London 1979, p. 17.

37. Michaela von Freyhold (1975), op. cit., p. 13-14.

38. Tanganyika Government, Annual Reports of the Labour Department, DSM, 1944.

39. A. Tambila, A History of the Tanga Sisal Labour Force, 1939-64, UDSM, M. A. Thesis, 1974, p. 102.

40. GTZ, Lower Mkomazi Irrigation Project, Tanzania Feasibility Study, Main Report, Eschborn 1982, p. 60.

41. Tambila, op. cit., p. 98.

42. H. O. Kaya, Effectiveness of the Existing Sisal-Based Industries in Reducing the Market Dependence of the Sisal Industry in Tanzania: A Case Study of the Tanga Region Industries, UDSM, 1978, pp. 57-77.

43. A. C. Mascarenhas, op. cit., p. 252.

44. Tanzania Sisal Corporation Act, Bill Supplement No. 5 to the Gazette of the United Republic of Tanzania, 27th October, 1967, p. 244.

45. P. Lawrence, The Sisal Industry of Tanzania. A Review of the Informal Commodity Agreement and Related Questions of Strategy, ERB, Paper 71.9.1971, p. 7.

46. Ndawula Kajumba, Socio-Economic Aspects of an African Plantation System, Tanzanian Sisal Plantation Case, ERB, UDSM, Jan. 1977, p. 12.

47. Master-Rolls are registers showing the particulars of the labourer such as name, date of birth, place of birth etc.

48. National Provident Fund is money deducted from a worker's wage every month and paid to him when he stops working.

49. ILO, Unemployment and Structural Change, Geneva 1962, p. 52; also see W. F. Maunder, Employment in an Underdeveloped Area, New Haven, Yale University Press 1972, p. 12.

50. Observation during the Field-Study and Interview with the TSA Statistician at the TSA Head Office, Tanga.

51. S. Kajumba, op. cit., p. 14.

52. G. W. Guillebaud, op. cit., p. 89.

53. Tanzania Sisal Authority, Annual Labour Reports, Tanga 1980.

54. N. Kajumba, op. cit., p. 21.

55. Interview with the TSA Personnel Officer, Head Office, Tanga.

56. Interview with the District Development Agricultural Officer, Korogwe.

57. Interview with the randomly selected labourers in the Plantations visited.

58. Daily News Paper, 17th April, 1978, p. 1, and 13th June, 1978, p. 1. This is the official government Newspaper in Tanzania.

59. Interview with the randomly selected labourers in the Plantations and with Omari Mbelwa and Said Chomoka at Mkalamo. The latter are the oldest people who live in a village near the Toronto Sisal Estate, Korogwe District.

60. Fuggles Couchman, <u>Agricultural Change in Tanzania</u>, Stanford Food Research Institute 1970, p. 26.

61. Interview with the Senior Economist of the Tanzania Sisal Authority (TSA), Head Office, Tanga.

62. P. R. Lawrence, <u>Plantation Sisal. The Inherited Mode of Production</u>, in <u>Lionel Cliffe</u> (ed.), <u>Rural Cooperation in Tanzania</u>, TPH, DSM, 1978, pp. 3-7.

63. N. Kajumba, op. cit., p. 3.

64. National Development Corporation, <u>JENGA</u>; DSM, No. 8, 1970, p. 34.

65. NUTA is the only Trade Union in Tanzania.

66. H. Mapolu, <u>The Organisation and Participation of Workers in Tanzania</u>, in Journal of African Politics, Development and International Affairs, Vol. 2, 3(1972), p. 400.

67. See the Nationalist Newspaper, 9th October, 1970, and the Presidential Circular on Workers Participation in Management, 1970.

68. The Standard Newspaper of 24th May, 1971.

69. H. Mapolu, op. cit., p. 403.

70. J. K. Nyerere, <u>Arusha Declaration</u>, DSM, Government Printer, 1967, p. 8.

71. TANU Guidelines (Mwongozo), DSM, 1972, paragraph 11.

72. R. F. Hopkins, <u>Socialism and Participation: Tanzania's 1970 National Election</u>, DSM, 1972. Also see H. Kjekshus, <u>The Question Hour in Tanzania's Bunge</u>, DSM, 1972.

73. A. J. Temu, <u>Public Involvement in Planning and Development in Tanzania</u>, University of York, Sept. 1973.

74. Sharon Stichter, op. cit., p. 30.

75. O. F. Raum, op. cit., p. 190.

76. Michaela von Freyhold (1975), op. cit., p. 10.

77. Tanganyika Government, <u>Annual Report of the Provincial Commissioner</u>, Tanga 1939, p. 92.

V. PEASANTS VERSUS GOVERNMENT

Chapter Four examined in a historical perspective the response of the local peasantry in the Tanga region to wage labour in the sisal plantations. This Chapter will investigate their reaction to the different government rural development programmes, which include export-crops production, village settlement policies and cooperative movements.

The previous chapter began with an examination of the different theories concerning wage labour in Africa. This chapter will also begin with an examination of the relevant literature pertaining to the peasantry in Africa south of the Sahara.

5.1. Theories on the African Peasantry

The literature on the question of rural socio-economic relations in Africa is quite extensive. Teodor Shanin defines peasants as:
> "those whose ultimate security and subsistence lies in their having certain rights in land and in the labour of family members on the land, but who are involved, through rights and obligations, in a wider economic system which includes the participation of non-peasants." 1

The above implies that the dependence of the peasant's security on maintaining rights in land and rights in family labour is an important determinant shaping and restricting their social actions.

Goran Hyden argues that Africa is the only continent where the peasants have not yet been captured by other social classes. By being owners of their own means of production, the smallholder peasants in Africa have enjoyed a degree of independence from the other social classes. He gives the following unique characteristics of the African peasantry:

(a) with the exception of South Africa and Zimbabwe, the economies of most of the African countries south of Sahara are dominated by the rural smallholder producers. Their contribution to Gross Domestic Product is generally large. The exact importance of the peasantry to economic development is difficult to measure in quantitative terms because what they produce and exchange is not registered.

(b) their income disparities are not due to ownership of land being in the hands of a few people. It is a matter of differential in using the land. African agriculture is still carried with rudimentary technology. The farms are small because of the limits imposed by the productive forces.

(c) agriculture in Africa is essentially rainfed. The mutual dependence on a key productive resource such as an irrigation canal, as in Asian countries is very limited. Farming is still dependent on natural resource endowment and on human labour. However, compared to his Asian counterpart the African peasant is socially more independent. In countries of Asia such as Bangladesh, a combination of overpopulation and skewed land distribution leave the majority of the peasants to exist on holdings which are far below their subsistence needs.

(d) given their rudimentary technology producing the basic necessities is a cumbersome task. The peasants invest so much time and effort in it that he is reluctant to take chances. The latter includes adopting innovations, even if they hold out the promise of financial gains.

(e) compared to Latin America peasants, the African peasants are less integrated in the cash economy. Although they have to sell some of their crops in order to acquire other necessities, the majority of the rural producers in Africa still subsist without much dependence on inputs from other sectors.

(f) as a social class the peasantry in Africa is the creation of colonialism. It is still in the making.[2] This is supported by Ken Post who states that the rural producers in most parts of Africa are still in the process of becoming peasants, i.e. they are transcending the boundary between 'primitive cultivators' and peasants. The number of those who are turning into capitalist farmers or labourers is still small. According to his analysis the principal feature of rural Africa is 'peasantization'. He is against those scholars[3] who talk of 'proletarianization' of the rural producers in Africa. John C. de Wilde observed that the smallproducer in Africa devotes approximately 60 to 70 per cent of his time to subsistence production.[4]

Goran Hyden's argument on the independence of the African peasantry from other classes fails to take into consideration the fact that although the peasant in Africa owns his means of production and is self-employed, he is nevertheless subjected to exploitation. In most African countries the people who exploit others do not necessarily own the means of production as individuals. They are able to exploit because they have access to state power. They use state power to control the means of production. The state forces the peasants to produce export crops like cotton, coffee, tea etc. and then sets itself up as the sole authorized buyer of these crops. It buys the crops cheaply from the peasant producers and sells them to European and American

importers at much higher prices. It retains the difference
instead of passing it on to the peasant producers.

In their discussion of the autonomy and dependence of the
peasantry in Africa, John Saul and Roger Woods point out
that the peasants stand somewhere between the 'primitive
agriculturalists' and the capitalist farmer. With the former
they share the notion of rights to land and the reliance
on family labour for security and subsistence. But like
the capitalist farmer the peasant is integrated into a
complex and differentiated society, in which demands can
be placed upon him.[5] Eric Wolf adds that it is the peasant's
exposure to regular extraction of a surplus of his production that distinguishes him from the 'primitive agriculturalist'.[6]

In her examination of the systems of production of the
African cultivator, Marilyn Silberfein argues that most
of the traditional agricultural systems devised by the
African cultivators were efficient in terms of the relationship of energy input to food-output. The cultivators were
well informed decision makers, utilizing a cumulative knowledge of the local environment and methods that have evolved
through centuries of trial and error. This combination
of information and techniques was expected to minimise
risk at predetermined work levels.[7] For example the system
of intercropping is conducive to the sequential maturation
of crops, which spreads out the harvesting efforts and
allows food to be available over a longer period of time.[8]
Moreover, intercropping provides a means of retarding the
spread of plant-specific pests, creates a dense network
of plants to hold down the penetration of weeds and allows
each crop to utilize its own specific soil nutrient requirements.[9] Furthermore, the canopy-effect such as the
planting together of banana and coffee trees is another

strategy of the farming system of the African cultivator, whereby taller plants (banana trees) provide shade and all the layers of the crop complex can retard erosion of the soil by reducing the impact of rainfall on the ground.

However, studies made by the Food and Agricultural Organisation of the United Nation (FAO) have shown that despite that per capita cultivable land is higher in Africa compared to the densely parts of Asia, labour inputs tend to be lower and soils are generally poorer. Hence, average per hectare yield of principal crops are lower in Africa than those attained in Asia.[10]

In order to increase productivity in the rural areas, the African governments use numerous strategies: One of these strategies is to try to reach the peasants by creating new village settlement schemes, i.e. new locations of both habitation and production. Examples of these new settlements are the villages of the transformation approach in the 1960s and the current 'Ujamaa Villages', both in Tanzania. These will be discussed later.

According to D. Leonard, the idea behind these new settlements is that, by placing the peasant producers in totally new surroundings, their local know-how will be invalid and they will consequently be more open to new ideas and methods of production. Moreover, through control of distribution of inputs, government officials hope to direct the peasants towards productivity.[11] Whether this strategy has been so far successful or not will be seen in our examination of the Tanzanian experience and Tanga region in particular.

Another policy tool common among most governments in Africa to encourage higher production from the rural areas is to raise the producer prices. The policy presupposes that the market is a significant factor for influencing peasant behaviour. However, experience has shown that the prime beneficiaries for these policies are those already absorbed in the market economy. These are much more sensitive to market mechanisms.[12]

5.2. Tanga Region Experiences

The past section made a general investigation of the different theories concerning the African peasantry, especially in relation to government demands on them to increase production. The following sections will try to examine these theories in relation to the peasants in Tanzania, particularly in the Tanga region.

5.2.1. Background to Peasant Export-Production

Peasant export production in the Tanga region did not begin with colonialism. The latter integrated the region more in the world market by introducing new export crops such as cotton, coffee, tea etc. for peasant production including new methods of production to suit the interests of the colonial countries. V. Harlow shows that there were already two types of trade existing in the region at the time of colonial establishment, i.e. the big and small caravan trades.
The big caravan trade was dominated by the coastal people: Arabs, Indians and Swahili. The common types of Arabs along the coast of Tanga during this time were the Maskata and Hadramant, who are commonly known by the local people in the region as 'Washihiri'. The only tribe in the hinterland of Tanga which took direkt part in the big caravan trade were the Zigua from Handeni. The traded commodities

included ivory, slaves, hippoteeth, rhinohorns, timber and rubber.
The small caravan trade involved agricultural products produced in the hinterland and along the coast of Tanga. The products of both the big and small caravan trades were exported mainly to Zanzibar through the ports of Tanga, Moa and Pangani.[13] For instance, the main products exported to Zanzibar from the Usambara Mountains were tobacco, butter, cattle, goats, sheep and honey (see Tables 5.1 and 5.2).

Table 5.1: The Value of Products from the Usambara exported through the Port of Tanga in the Period 1888/89 and 1889/90

Product	(Value in German Marks) 1888/89	1889/90
Butter	785	1,744
Cattle	436	175
Goats/Sheep	35	1,362
Honey	393	446
Total	1,649	3,727

Source: Karl Garger, Tangaland und die Kolonisation Deutsch-Ostafrika - Tatsachen und Vorschläge, Berlin 1898, p. 25.

Table 5.2: Value of Products from the Usambaras exported through Pangani Port

Product	(Value in German Marks) 1888/89	1889/90
Butter	38,778	33,665
Cattle	5,865	6,190
Goats/Sheep	5,334	8,830
Total	49,977	48,685

Source: Karl Garger, op. cit., p. 26.

Pangani was the most important port für die export of butter, cattle, sheep and goats from the Usambaras. The Arabs and Swahili people along the coast of Tanga had sugar cane and coconut plantations based on slave labour. Coconut palms were widely spread along the coast and inland along the Pangani river to the Wami river, and north of the Usambaras till Daluni. It is estimated that at the time of German colonial establishment, there were about 80,000 coconut trees in the region.

The coconut product had different uses: as a food crop and as export crop. For trading purposes the nut is dried and is known as copra. The leaves are known in Kiswahili as 'Makuti' and are used for making mats and for thatching houses. Another important crop at the coast was cassava. It produces even in baren land and hence very conducive in the dry areas of the region. The Digo and Segeju people who are recent converts from pastorism to crop cultivators due to Masai raids of their cattle, adopted cassava as their main staple food and cash crop. They sold some of it to Zanzibar. Other important crops exportet to Zanzibar were sesam, sorghum, rice and tobacco.[14]

The trade in grain between the ports of Tanga and Pangani and the inland people was controlled by Indians. The Indians either bought the products themselves from the inland people or sometimes brought their products themselves to the Indian shops in Tanga, Pangani, Tongani, Doda and Moa along the coast. The Indians brought the grains cheaply in big containers from the producers and sold it expensively to foreign traders in small containers called 'vibaba' in Swahili.

Along the coast money in form of rupees, copper pieces and 'Maria Theresianthala' or 'reali' were used. In the interior goods were mainly exchanges by barter system. European and Asian goods were used such as 'Marikani' (a white cloth) and 'Leso' (coloured cloth). The Digo and Segeju people along the coast used a black cloth known as 'Kaniki' in Kiswahili and the inland peoples, i.e. Zigua, Shambaa and Bondei used the white cloth (Merikani).[15]

During the early stages of German colonial establishment in the region, the colonialists cultivated the same crops grown by the local people. In 1909 Governor von Rechenberg issued the following statements:

> "Rohstofflieferung an Deutschland ..., auf dieses Ziel kommt es an ... und erst in zweiter Linie, ob es durch Plantagenanbau oder Eingeborenen-Kultur erreicht wird ..." 16

The above statement reflected the two ways in which agricultural materials could be exploited, i.e. through European controlled plantations using african cheap labour and through introduction of peasant export-crop production grown by a family or the whole tribe. The marketing of which was to be under European or Indian control. Among the agricultural products which were highly demanded in Germany at the time were cotton, rubber and sisal. A consumer product which was demanded was coffee.[17] Colonial

Germany was not necessarily interested in these products because they were cheap, but because of their strategic importance. The industries which required them were of such importance to the economy for political and military reasons. Therefore, Germany required an independent source of these products which she could effectively control. For instance she wanted to produce cotton in the then German East Africa to reduce the risk of price fluctuations brought about by the American suppliers. An independent supply of these commodities would also ease her foreign exchange requirements. It was for these reasons that a large quantity of the products produced in German East Africa were exported to Germany itself as shown in Table 5.3.

Table 5.3: Principal Total Exports sent to Germany from German East Africa in 1911 (Value in Thousands of Marks)

Item	Total Exports	Exports to Germany
Rubber	8,391	6,050
Sisal fibre	4,532	4,423
Hides and Skins	3,035	237
Copra	1,848	185
Coffee	1,266	561
Gold	1,023	1,013
Beewax	817	452
Timber	515	460
Ivory	405	14
Mica	348	348
Gum Copal	107	13
Wattle and Bark	96	27
Total	21,532	12,938

Source: M. J. Yaffey, International Transactions Before and During the German Period, DSM, ERB (Mimeo), 1967, p. 8.

Coffee was introduced in the Usambaras basically as a
European settlers crop. Its cultivation as a peasant cash
crop has not been much of a success because the soil became
too quickly exhausted and acidic. Large amounts of manure
and chemical inputs are required to keep up yields. Later
coffee was replaced by tea which grows better on acidic
soils. But the latter is limited to certain altitudes and
the peasants complain that it requires a lot of labour.[18]
Sisal was introduced as a plantation crop (see Part 4.2.1.).

As a result of the dry climatic conditions in most parts
of Handeni district and the north-eastern parts of Korogwe,
cotton was introduced to enable the peasant farmers to
earn cash income and pay taxes and create a market for
industrial goods from the metropole.

In both the German and British colonial periods force was
used to make the peasants grow cotton. The work of enforcing its cultivation was entrusted to the village chiefs.
The Zigua people in Handeni and other parts of the region
where the crop was enforced were used to a limited number
of crops using their traditional methods of cultivation.
The cultivation of traditional crops such as sorghum, beans,
sweet potatoes etc. was found easy and of direct benefit
to the peasant himself and his family. Cotton was a new
crop and its cultivation under new methods was found to
be too demanding. The new crop needed early performance
of the following activities: preparation of the field,
sowing of the seeds, weeding, reduction of plants, spraying, harvest etc. The peasants were forced to follow these
procedures. Those who failed to do so were imprisoned or
fined. Others were prosecuted for not being present in
their fields during the 'normal' cultivation hours. There was
resistance against the cultivation of the crop and the
chiefs who enforced development.[19]

5.2.2. The Post-independence Peasant Agricultural Production

5.2.2.1. The Transformation and Improvement Approaches

The transition to independence in Tanzania mainland coincided with a visit by a World Bank Mission entrusted to look into the future of the country's economy. In the case of the agricultural sector it recommended the following:

> "Something more is required, whether through intensive campaigns in settled areas, involving a variety of co-ordinated measures, or through planned and supervised settlement of areas which are at present uninhabited or thinly inhabited ... the Mission judges that the second of these approaches is in general the more promising in the present conditions of Tanganyika." 20

The final decision on the above recommendation was left to the new government. During the early years of independence Tanzania like other new states of Africa, policy making was a trial and error process. The incoming political leaders had no sense of constraints. According to them independence gave Tanzania a chance to start a new. They were anxious to seize on everything that looked like an untapped opportunity. The result of which was an uncritical approach to policy-making.[21] Therefore in 1962 the new government approved the World Bank's recommendation to 'transform' peasant agriculture through settlement schemes. This was after a year of failure of the early post independence People's Plan, which aimed at establishing independent village schemes in the hope that through the declaration of independence a spirit of self-help would develop in the rural areas. In the Tanga region the first people to respond to these early schemes were members of the TANU Young League. The schemes became unseccessful because of limited extension manpower and the conflict between the old village leaders and the new Party leaders.[22] This failure led to a shift of emphasis from the self help and voluntary labour schemes to national building projects. The transformation approach meant setting up new farms and recruiting farmers willing to go there. It was hoped that by taking the people out of their traditional social environment they would be more open to change and the government would be able to exercise control over the settlements. They would be supervised by government-appointed managers and thus the authorities would have access to the farmers in a way that was not possible with smallholder peasants scatterd over large areas.

A Rural Settlement Commission with a Village Settlement Agency as its executive section was established. The responsibility of the latter was to supervise the settlement schemes and advise the government on matters relating to their implementation. A number of ex-colonial administration were appointed to occupy senior positions in the Agency.

The first government planned settlements were set up in various parts of the country. The First Five Year Development Plan of 1964 recommended the establishment of over 69 such model villages schemes. Settlers were recruited from areas with land shortage like the Usambara Mountains in the Tanga region and Kilimanjaro region. Some of them came from the urban unemployed.
The new areas were opened up with the assistance of mechanized equipment, and the settlers were invited to build houses and start farming on plots allocated to them. Settling was often a difficult process for them, especially those from the mountain areas who were used to different climates and soils. Moreover, they did not know each other and establishment of a new social organization was characterised by tension. At the beginning the government pro-

vided them with food rations, when they were unable to produce their own food.[23] H. Newinger who also made an evaluation of the Villagization Policies of the 1960s in Tanzania argues that the principal problems of these settlements was related to government supervision and aid. Agricultural production was carried out with farm machinery of which the settlers were expected eventually to repay the capital costs involved in establishing their farms.[24] Most of the studies made on these schemes criticized the overcapitalization which characterized them, i.e. there was more machinery than necessary in relation to land and labour available.[25]

I. Bavu gives the example of the settlement scheme at Kabuku in Handeni District, which was established in collaboration with the Amboni Sisal Estates as a cooperative sisal plantation. The government did not take into account of the differences between the form of production practised on the existing large-scale sisal plantations in Amboni and that of the new settlement schemes. Imitation of the former type of production meant the introduction of expensive heavy equipment like bulldozers for bush clearing. As a result the new settlers started off with a large debt of 2.5 million Tanzanian shillings, part of which had to be paid by the government.[26]

René Dumont adds that the settlement schemes of the transformation approach created a group of semi-privileged people who were under little pressure to work due to an excessive degree of mechanization.[27] However, this argument is not accepted by the settlers themselves. For instance, the settlers at Kabuku argued that the machinery made them work more than peasants in other parts of the country. Moreover, they claimed to have had less time to look after their own household needs and felt deprived of autonomy that their relatives and friends outside the settlement enjoyed. When the supervisors of the Amboni estates told them that they were producing far less sisal than workers in the Amboni estates and that absenteeism was a common problem, their counter argument was that they were peasants and not workers.[28] Tensions between the government officials and the settlers at Kabuku were quite common during the early years of the settlements. Later the government decided to eliminate the Village Settlement Agency. Supervision of the schemes by the government staff was terminated and mangerial responsibilities were shared between the settlers themselves and the Amboni Sisal Estates. This gave the settlers an autonomy and a chance to diversify their production to other products especially food crops like maize and sorghum. Their commitment to produce sisal declined because of the fluctuating world market prices of the commodity.[29]

Nevertheless, the government's efforts to improve traditional peasant agriculture were not abandoned because of the attention given to the transformation approach in the first five years of independence. Agricultural training was also strongly emphasized during the early 1960s. Institutions known as Farmers' Training Centres (FTC) were established. There is no evidence that these FTCs really reached the peasant farmers. Most of the participants were those peasants who showed interests in 'modern' farming techniques, i.e. the progressive farmers.

The Party and government did not want to take unpopular measures against the peasants. For instance popular demands wanted the government to do the following: remove poll tax, nullify ordinances prohibiting settlement on forest reserves, do away with all agricultural regulations etc. The government took a soft approach to these demands,

i.e. through persuasion. The results of this government
approach were that people felt free to ignore the different
agricultural regulations introduced. For example in the
Usambara Mountains where there is a shortage of land, people
began to clear forest areas for cultivation.
In areas where new crops were introduced and they signi-
fied a major gain to producers without disturbing their
traditional livelihoods, agricultural extension service
was able to achieve some results. Poul Westergaard gives
the example of the Makonde peasants in Mtwara region, where
the government introduced the production of cashew nuts
during the early 1960s through persuasion. The new crop
did not impose any great demands for labour. The main task
apart from harvesting was weeding the land.[30]

However J. Gus Liebenow points out that government's efforts
to encourage the Makonde peasants to grow rice in the Ruvuma
river valley with the aid of mechanized equipment were
rejected by the peasants due to the excessive labour demands
that mechanized rice cultivation imposed.[31] These examples
demonstrate that it is sometimes easy to introduce a new
crop but more difficult to introduce new production practices among the peasants.

The results of these policies were that the government
decided to leave the majority of the peasants untouched
and concentrated its extension services and inputs on those
interested in 'modern' farming. It was assumed that the
best farmers in each village community would encourage
their neighbours to improve, i.e. their achievements would
have a demonstration effect.[32] Furthermore, J. H. Konter
who made an analysis of the peasant economy in Rungwe district (Southwestern Tanzania) argues that agricultural
extension staff tend to be confined to the 'progressive'
farmers because the ordinary peasants are not seeking

their cooperation. They know that getting involved with
the extension staff is the beginning of a relationship
that may lead to government intervention in their farming.[33]

5.2.2.2. Rural Development Through Socialism and Self-reliance

The redefinition of rural development policy followed the
formulation in February 1967 of the Arusha Declaration.
Its two fundamental principles were 'socialism' and self-
reliance. In the case of rural development self-reliance
meant freedom to implement development projects without
depending on aid from the government. Socialism meant the
absence of exploitation, corruption and class division in
society. The most important part of the new approach was
the creation of cooperative and communal villages known
as 'Ujamaa villages'. According to President Nyerere's
explanation the basis of 'Ujamaa' policy lies in a synthesis
of the old and new style of life:
> "... the traditional African family lived according
> to the basic principles of Ujamaa ... They lived together
> and worked together because this was how they under-
> stood life and how they reinforced each other against
> difficulties they had to contend with ... The results
> of their efforts were divided equally between them,
> but according to well understood customs ..." [34]

The peasants' conception of 'Ujamaa' differed from the
official view. It was interpreted from the side of its
effects on the peasant household. Therefore the same appre-
hension which the peasants had when the 1962 Land Tenure
Act was announced reappeared. People believed that they
would lose their land. In the case of the Arusha Declaration
rumours spread that the peasants would lose their land,
wives and children.[35] In respect to the use of force in
the establishment of the 'Ujamaa villages' President Nyerere
said the following:

"Ujamaa Villages ... cannot be created from outside
nor governed from outside. No one can be forced into
an Ujamaa village, and no official at any level can
tell the members of an Ujamaa village what they should
do ... For if these things happen ... then it will no
longer be an Ujamaa village." 36

The first two years after the Arusha Declaration saw a
limited development of the 'Ujamaa villages' in the country.
The first people to respond to the call were TANU Youth
League groups who initiated 'Ujamaa villages' or transformed
their existing settlements into communal villages. Some
of the former village settlement schemes also declared
themselves to be 'Ujamaa villages'. An example of the latter
is the Kabuku-Ndani in Handeni district.[37]
It was a result of this slow development that in 1970 to
1971 the Party began to take a more active role in the
creation of 'Ujamaa villages'. The President took a personal
lead by initiating 'Operation Dodoma'.[38] Table 5.4 shows
the quantitative development of the new villages in the
country.

By 1973 over 2 million Tanzanians were reported to live
in the 'Ujamaa villages'. Table 5.5 shows the development
of the 'Ujamaa villages' in the districts of the Tanga
region.

There were essentially four methods through which the 'ujamaa villages' in the region were established: transforming
former settlement schemes; encouraging traditional villages
to begin cooperative activities; voluntary establishment
by the peasants themselves; and those established by government authorities mostly by force.
In the Usambara Mountains most of the 'Ujamaa villages'
were established through reorganising the traditional villages and encouraging them to begin coooperative activities.
The starting point of the new villages in the Usambara
was communal production of vegetables on a plot allocated
to them by the village committee.

Table 5.4: Chronological Development of 'Ujamaa Villages' in Tanzania

Date	Number of Ujamaa Villages	Total Population of the Villages	Total population as % of nation
Feb. 1967	50	5,000	0.04
Dec. 1968	180	59,000	0.5
Jul. 1969	480	-	-
Dec. 1969	650	150,000	1.1
Jul. 1970	1,180	-	-
Dec. 1970	1,630	530,000	4
Jun. 1971	2,670	840,000	6
Dec. 1971	4,480	1,600,000	12
May. 1973	5,630	2,030,000	15
Jul. 1975	8,020	11,200,000	70
Jun. 1980	10,200	15,660,000	87

Source: A. Ellman, Progress and Prospects in Ujamaa Development in Tanzania, ERB (Mimeo), DSM, 1981

Table 5.5: Development of 'Ujamaa Villages' in the Tanga Region

District	Number of Ujamaa Villages			
	1970	1972	1975	Febr. 1983
Handeni	9	48	96	102
Korogwe	3	59	78	115
Lushoto	5	45	67	85
Pangani	7	32	25	52
Muheza	8 [a]	30 [a]	37	35
Tanga			6	10
Total	32	214	309	399

[a] = Until 1972 Muheza and Tanga formed one district (Tanga rural and urban).

Source: Regional 'Ushirika' Office, Tanga

In Muheza district 'Ujamaa' was initially welcomed by members of the TANU Youth League and by ex-sisal workers. In Pangani the promise of government aid led peasants to start voluntarily 'Ujamaa' activities in agriculture and fisheries. In the Korogwe district about 85 % of the villages were established by reorganising old villages and encouraging them to begin cooperative activities.[39]

5.2.2.3. Limitations of Ujamaa Development and New Approach to Agricultural Production

Although the quantitative implications of the operations and campaigns to start the 'Ujamaa villages' were quite impressive (see Table 5.4), it is significant to recognize that the figures conceal important variations:

(i) villages were registered even if their communal efforts were not successful. For instance out of the 115 registered villages in the Korogwe district in 1983, only one village had reached stage three of 'Ujamaa' development in which all the economic activities are done communally. This village is Magamba-Kwalukonge in Mombo division. The village was formed by ex-sisal workers. In this village economic activities like agriculture, small-scale industries, village shop are run communally. The villagers have a sisal estate, a lorry and a passenger bus. Moreover, the 20/= Tanzanian shillings which every pupil in Tanzania has to pay as school fees are paid in this village for every pupil by the village council.

(ii) not all the villages were new creations. People were in some cases told to move to the nearest existing village or trading centre, and then political efforts were made to create an 'Ujamaa village' out of the enlarged unit.

(iii) communal production was introduced as a complement to individual production. Many small capitalist farmers participated in communal production although their dependence on it was very small.[40]

(iv) the policy of village concentrations was by no means new in Tanzania when it was announced in 1967. It has been followed by the colonial regimes and it had also been an integral part of TANU policy in the early post-independence years. The 'Ujamaa' approach was unique in that it was meant to neutralize the powers of the small capitalist farmers and enable the smallholder producers to participate effectively in the construction of a socialist economy.[41] But the 'Ujamaa' village programme disappointed its early proponents by failing to gain ideological acceptance among the peasantry. Most of the rural people reacted to it with a set of attitudes that ranged from scepticism and mistrust to out right resentment. President Nyerere himself acknowledged this reaction by accepting the use of coercion in moving peasants to new village settlements.[42]

(v) the work of convincing the peasants on the advantages of 'socialism' was entrusted to administrators and field staff who had been in charge of the implementation of previous government policies including colonial policies. It was expected that a number of seminars and Party directives would transform these functionaries into cadres who could plan and stimulate socialist production and attitudes among the peasants. By 1973 only 14 % of the population of the country had moved into new villages. Official figures reveal that out of more than 5000 villages established in 1974 only 8 % had reached stage three of Ujamaa development in which collective farming assumes a major economic significance.[43] In his examination of the relationship between 'socialism and traditional African societies', I. Kopytoff argues that cooperation may exist between limited social groups like the family, age groups etc. for certain activities, but the establishment of socialism needs more than extending the boundaries of family co-operation to larger groups. This is because such extension does not take place in a vacuum. It involves overcoming other socio-economic obstacles which characterised the previous modes of life.[44]

In Korogwe and Handeni districts the 'Ujamaa' movement was haunted from the beginning by the following problems:

(vi) there were numerous occasions in which peasants were moved from their traditional residences to the new areas in the midst of planting, growing or harvesting period. The result of which were that entire crops were lost because of poor timing by the local officials. Furthermore, the officials and the peasants themselves were not certain on how long the newly settled villages would require to become ready to resume production. The settling process was even longer for villagers who had been reallocated to a different ecological milieu, where they had to become accustomed to cultivating under new conditions.

(vii) By initially stressing the primacy of hoe cultivation in the villages, the authorities concerned with 'Ujamaa' development left the productive forces untouched, with the exception of work organization. In his study of the 'Village Technology for Rural Development in Tanzania', George Macpherson argues that very little attention was given to the peasants' working equipment in the 'Ujamaa villages'. Improved seeds, irrigation, fertilizers, pesticides and land reforms have all received much theoretical and sometimes practical considerations. But the peasants' tools have relatively been neglected. He further says that this neglection arises from the fact that most of the government authorities concerned with rural development suppose that the problem of better tools for the peasantry in the developing countries has already been solved for them in the industrialized countries. The task for each developing country is to chose from the manufacturer's catalogue the appropriate technology for its peasantry.[45]

(viii) given the dependence of Tanzanian agriculture on rain, especially in semi-arid areas like Handeni, timing of all farming activities is very vital. Everything has to be done within the span of a few days. Therefore the introduction of communal farms by the government side by side with the private household plots brought organisational complications for the peasants. Peasants prefered to give first attention to their private farms, over which they had direct control. Most of the studies of 'Ujamaa' development conclude that output on the communal farms has been below that on the private farms.[46] Table 5.6 shows a comparison of cotton production from 'Ujamaa' and private farms as percentages of total production in the Korogwe district.

Table 5.6 shows that the area of cotton cultivation under Ujamaa farming has been increasing over the period shown and that under private farming has been fluctuating. But it is also seen that during the same period more cotton was produced in the private farms than in the communal farms. In the period 1981 and 1982 there was more hectarage under communal farming because of the government's campaigns to force peasants in the district to grow more cotton in the 'Ujamaa farms'.

Table 5.6: <u>Cotton Production on Ujamaa and Private Farms in the Korogwe District as Percentages of Total Production (Ares in Hectares and Output in Tons)</u>

Item		1979	1980	1981	1982
Ujamaa (1)	(A)	80	107	164	204
Production	(O)	4.6	6.1	11.8	15.7
Private (2)	(A)	113	115	103	126
Production	(O)	8.5	12.6	15.0	20.8
Total (3)	(A)	193	222	267	330
Production	(O)	13.1	18.7	26.8	36.0
(1) as % of (3)	(A)	41.5	48.2	64.1	61.8
	(O)	35.1	32.6	44.0	42.2
(2) as % of (3)	(A)	58.5	51.8	38.6	38.2
	(O)	64.9	67.4	56.0	57.8

A = Area   O = Output

Source: District Agricultural Office, <u>Annual Production Reports</u>, Korogwe

(ix) although the Party emphasizes that political leadership of the new villages should be under the ordinary peasants, as a result of democratic elections the rich peasants often end up to be village leaders.

Peasants often chose petty bourgeoisie to head their
villages on the assumption that they were the most
able to deal with government officials, including
protecting them from government interventions. In
places where there are no such petty bourgeoisie,
they chose individuals who were not interested in
change. They deliberately elected someone who would
not interfere in their daily life.[47] In Handeni dis-
tric, examples of such cases of leaders were so frequent that the Party leadership had to increase its
scrutiny of the local leadership election process.[48]
Moreover, studies in the Tanga region have also shown
that some of the village leadership used their positions for their own benefits. In the Korogwe district, for instance, where more than 40 % of the
arable land is covered by sisal plantations, the
average size of land per family of four to five people
is between 0.5 to 1.0 hectare.[49] But during the field
study for this work, it was observed that in some
villages like Mkomazi, Mkumbara, Bagamoyo and Mheza,
all the village chairmen had more than 1.5 hectares
of land, and at one time or another of the agricultural production these leaders employ wage labour
to supplement their family labour. The main crop
grown in these villages is rice. It was also observed
that in Mkomazi and Bagamoyo the village chairmen
were former traditional chiefs of the areas.
Tables 5.7 und 5.8 show land distribution in the
Korogwe and Handeni districts among the households.

Table 5.7 shows that there is pressure of land in the
Korogwe district. An average of 48 % of the households
have land between 0.5 and 1.0 hectare. Only 1 % of them
have 3 hectares or over. This is because the best land
in the district is occupied by sisal plantations. According

Table 5.7: <u>Land Distribution in two Divisions of Korogwe
District (as % of total number of households)
(1982)</u>

Hecterage	Divisions	
	Mombo	Korogwe
0 - 0.5	15	25
0.5 - 1.0	45	50
1.0 - 1.5	20	9
1.5 - 2.0	10	7
2.0 - 2.5	7	5
2.5 - 3.0	2	3
3.0 and over	1	1

Source: District Agricultural Development Office, Korogwe, 1982

Table 5.8: <u>Land Distribution in 7 Divisions of Handeni
District (% of total households) (1982)</u>

Hecterage	Chani-ka	Kwe-viku	Sin-deni	Mzundu	Mkum-buru	Magam-ba	Kim-be
0 - 0.5	15	5	3	2	10	4	15
0.5 - 1.0	30	25	25	30	20	20	25
1.0 - 1.5	13	15	18	20	16	10	10
1.5 - 2.0	26	30	35	30	28	34	30
2.0 - 2.5	8	12	8	7	14	15	10
2.0 - 3.0	5	10	7	6	8	5	7
3.0 and over	3	3	4	5	4	2	2

Source: District Agricultural Development Office, Handeni, 1982

to the District Development Director in Korogwe, sisal plantations occupy about 43 % of the cultivatable land in the district.
Table 5.8 indicates that there is less pressure for land in Handeni. This is because the district is less affected by sisal plantations compared to Korogwe. The district is also the largest in the region and is sparsely populated (see Chapter III, Section 3.5).
About 30 % of the households in the district have land size between 1.5 and 2.0 hectares. The main constraint for Handeni is the dry weather conditions and poor farming methods, otherwise the farms would have been large. Currently vast amounts of land lie unutilized.

In the Handeni district it is not the scarcity of land which is the main constraint for the expansion of the farmed areas. The main reason for the small sizes of the farms is due to poor climatic conditions especially the unreliability of the rainfall. The level of agricultural equipment also limits expansion of the farms.
Most of the 'Ujamaa' development initiatives in the villages have so far been coming from the government authorities. The villagers have defined 'Ujamaa' as something which the government authorities need. This is partly due to uneven distribution of knowledge between the villagers and the authorities.

1973 was a very significant year in the Post-Arusha developments. It was the beginning of a drought that greatly reduced Tanzania's grain harvest (see Table 5.9).
It was in the same year that President Nyerere announced that all Tanzanians in the rural areas would have to live in villages by the end of 1975, i.e. there was to be compulsory villagization in the country. Studies made on this villagization programme point out that it was the largest resettlement effort in the history of Africa.[50] In his

review of the achievements and problems after ten years
of Arusha Declaration, President Nyerere mentioned that
9.1 million people were moved into the new villages between
November 1973 and June 1975.[51] The mass resettlement
campaigns were organizsed on a regional or district basis.
People had to agree to leave their previous residences
and land and move to areas allocated by the government.
Where they refused to accept this condition force was applied.
Party and government authorities competed to prove
their capacity to mobilize the peasants. Existing government
programmes were abandoned in favour of villagization.
Army units were called in to supplement : the civilian personnel
and equipment. More than 80 % of the existing
registered villages in Handeni were established by force.
The scattered peasants had to respond to the programme.[52]
The reaction of the peasants to these measures was to resist
to move to the locations selected by the district
authorities, particularly where clan boundaries were not
considered, and where personal motives of the local leaders
were suspected. Later the Party had to intervene to stop
the use of force, but the peasants were never told that
the authorities had made a mistake. Therefore in retaliation,
some of them returned to their traditional villages.[53]

Furthermore, after the serious droughts that forced the
country to import large quantites of food after 1974,[54]
both the Party and government became seriously concerned
with food production. The government realized the difficulties
in purchasing grain from the peasants in times
of emergency. For instance the Daily News Paper of 20th
October, 1974, reported that inspite of appeals by the
government to the peasants to sell their 'surplus' grain
to the National Milling Corporation, the response was not
encouraging.[55] Therefore a variety of measures had to be
taken to cope up with the situation.

Table 5.9: <u>Annual Output of the Main Staple Grains in Tanzania (in Tons)</u>

Crop	1971	1973	1974	1975	1976	1977	1978	1979	1980
Maize	184,996	114,050	73,620	24,908	91,102	129,341	213,128	220,402	161,489
Paddy	93,495	73,094	59,702	23,603	18,344	23,278	53,957	52,224	42,528
Wheat	42,868	51,258	32,775	14,988	25,802	27,352	35,011	28,762	26,530

<u>Source</u>: Ministry of Agriculture, Maize, Paddy-rice, Wheat Annual Production Outputs, DSM, 1982.

Expansion of large-scale grain production on state farms in the different parts of the country as an alternative channel for the production of surplus grain. The management of these farms was to be in the hands of expatriates in the initial stages.[56]

Certain foreign donors proposed the improvement of farm and village storage facilities. In the Tanga region a project of constructing village stores has already started through the cooperation of the West German Technical Assistance, i.e. The Tanga Integrated Rural Development Programme (TIRDEP).

The distribution of the stores depends on the remoteness of the division and its production potentiality. Bungu division in the Korogwe district has more village stores than the other divisions because of its agricultural potentiality. A lot of export-crops are grown in this division like tea, coffee and cardamom. In Handeni the divisions of Kimbe and Kwekivu are the remotest in the district from the district headquarters at Chanika. The areas are also potential for the cultivation of food crops like maize, millet, cassava, beans and rice.

However the already constructed stores face the following constraints: the villagers demand payment for the self-help activities they render and are still reluctant to utilze the stores on the fear that their products will be stolen. Others do not want the government to know how much they have produced.[57]

Another measure taken by the government to encourage peasants to increase food production was to raise producer prices on all major grain crops. Table 5.10 shows the development of the official producer prices for maize and paddy.

Table 5.10: Official Producer Prices of Maize and Paddy (cents/kg)

Crop	1976	1977	1978	1979	1980	1981	1982
Maize	75-80	80	85	85	100	120	150
Paddy	100	100	120	120	150	175	250

Source: Regional Trade Office, Tanga, Febr. 1983

The policy of rising producer prices presupposes that the market is a significant factor in influencing peasant behaviour. This is questionable in an underdeveloped economy like that of Tanzania where peasants are only marginally incorporated into the capitalist economy and above all they have no control over the movement of the prices of the manufactured goods they have to buy with the money income they earn from the sale of the products.[58]

Moreover, even if prices are attractive there is a constraint in terms of what the household can produce with its available family labour. Table 5.11 shows the average family labour force and man/land ratios on individual farms in the Tanga region. The past argument does not mean that price incentives are absolutely ineffective, but they are not as important as is generally considered by the policy makers. As previously pointed out by David Leornard (see section 5.1) that if the price increases are marginal, the beneficiaries of the policy tend to be those producers who are already absorbed by the market economy, i.e. the small capitalist farmers.[59]

Inspite of the relatively big differences between the districts one can generally say that the labour force per household is comparatively small. Muheza and Lushoto districts had the highest man/land ratios. This is due to the small size of the individual farms.[60]

Table 5.11: <u>Family Labour Force and Man/Land Ratios on Individual Farms in the Tanga Region (1980)</u>

Item	Hande-ni	Korog-we	Lusho-to	Muhe-za	Panga-ni	Region
Average Number of Labourers per Household	2.4	2.3	2.2	1.9	1.6	2.1
Man/Land Ratio (Labour per hectare)	1:0.6	1:0.55	1:0.37	1:0.32	1:0.72	1:0.45

<u>Source:</u> Regional Agricultural Office, Tanga

Inspite of the relatively big differences between the districts, one can generally say that the labour force per household is comparatively small. Muheza and Lushoto districts had the highest man/land ratios. This is due to the small size of the individual farms.[60]
Furthermore, the government took the position that peasant agricultural production had to be increased at any cost. The form of production, i.e. whether communal or private became of secondary importance. There was no longer insistence on communal farming. Production on private holdings especially block farms was given priority. In August 1975 a new 'Villages and Ujamaa Villages Act' was announced. Based on this Act one or another form of block farming[61] was considered sufficient for a village to become officially identified as an 'Ujamaa Village'. The new villages

were not referred to as 'Ujamaa villages' but as 'planned' or 'development' villages.
The new Act went on to say that each village whether 'Ujamaa' or not will be registered as a separate legal entity which can undertake various economic activities and obtain funds from public and other sources. This was meant to encourage a certain amount of self-government in the villages by institutionalizing the Village Assembly. The latter consisted of all village members, as the ultimate authority, and the Village Council as its executive organ.[62]

Some recent studies have interpreted this modification of policy as a failure of the Party and government to bring about rural socialism in Tanzania. This is because the concept of 'Ujamaa' which was once intended to convey a social ideal of collective ownership has now been reduced to a state of affairs in which individual farming is intermittently supplemented by occasional cooperation in such tasks as planting and harvesting.[63] Moreover, most of the villages are still financially too weak to take full advantage of this new legislation. It was also in 1975 that the government decided to abolish all the primary cooperative societies in the country.

5.2.2.4. A Brief Historical Background of the Post-Independence Cooperative Societies

Marketing cooperative societies for agricultural products have existed in Tanzania since the 1920s, but it was after independence that their dominance in the rural sector has become significant. In 1952 there were 172 registered cooperative societies. When the country became independent in 1961 there were 857 of them. After the Arusha Declaration in 1967 the number had increased to 1650. The tonnage handled by these societies increased over four time since the early 1960s.[64]

In Tanzania like in other African countries after independence, cooperatives had the following significances: political leaders regarded them as one of the principal means of realizing 'African Socialism';[65] they were also a way of replacing non-African middlemen by Africans especially in the field of capital formation; as agencies of modernization they could help to bring the peasants into the monetary economy. It was believed that cooperatives give even the geographically most remote peasant an opportunity to sell what he produces. In addition, the government can reach the peasant through the cooperatives for educational purposes. The agricultural extension officers can also work through them;[66] in the colonial period development activities were directed and closely supervised by the government bureaucracy. Cooperatives allow the peasantry to participate in development.[67] Before their abolition in 1975, the cooperatives were organised as follows:
- At the lowest level of the structure was the primary society. This received the agricultural produce of its members, weighed it, bagged, paid for it, stored it (where necessary), ensured it and arranged for its transport to the market. At the same time it offered credit facilities, extended agricultural advice, distributed imports and provided other services.
Membership in these societies was open to everybody although there was overrepresentation of the rich farmers in the leadership and they often received special preferences in terms of credit and allowances.
The societies activities were financed by deductions or levies on the price paid to the producer. The deductions were calculated on a specific basis, i.e. a given amount of money per kilogramme of product handled. The deduction were approved by the meetings of the cooperative members.

The primary societies were themselves members of Cooperative Unions, of which there were 30 of them in the country in 1975. The Unions performed essentially the same functions as their primary societies but on a larger and more centralized basis. The principal function of the unions was to market the produce of their member societies. However, some primary societies did not belong to any union. For instance the pyrethrum societies sold their produce directly to the processors.
The Union activities were financed like those of the primary societies, i.e. by levies on the produce they handled. They also negotiated for local transport, bags, bank interests, insurance etc. The suppliers passed the costs on to the direct producer via further deductions from the price of his produce.

The next stage of agricultural marketing beyond the cooperative union were the Produce Marketing Boards. These are the current Crop Marketing Authorities like Cotton Authority, Coffee Authority etc. The Marketing Boards controlled in one way or another over 90 % of the total monetary output of the non-subsistence agricultural sector.[68] The present Crop Authorities are supposed to buy the produce from the villages or individual farmers at prices fixed by the government well in advance of each crop season, to transport the crops to the points of further processing or consumption (in the case of National Milling Corporation), to take responsibility from the necessary storage and to arrange any subsequent marketing of the final product. They are also responsible for the supply of the necessary input factors such as seeds, fertilizers, insecticides etc. for their respective crops. The latter is done in conjunction with the Regional Trading Companies (RTCs), Tanzania Rural Development Bank (TRDB) and other relevant public sector institutions. Although there are vast dif-

ferences with respect to the performance of the different
institutions, it is generally acknowledged that the operation of the Crop Authorities is not satisfactory. The
adequate supply of inputs at the required time is still
a great problem. This is much due to organisational short-
comings as to recurring problems of insufficient financial
liquidity of these institutions and to the general non-
availability of many important items as a result of the
extremely tight foreign exchange situation of the country.
The individual farmers and villages have no other potential
source for securing their supplies apart from the prescribed
public institutions. In respect to the marketing of different crops, the situation differs widely. In the case
of the typical export crops such as cotton, coffee etc.
there is no alternative available other than the marketing
monopoly of the respective crop authorities.

The situation is quite different when it comes to the marketing of food crops like maize or rice. These can be used
for domestic consumption and can be easily be marketed
in small quantities on any local market.[69] The low working
efficiency of the National Milling Corporation, especially
frequent lack of marketing and retail activities in the
rural areas as well as occasional shortages provide considerable opportunities for farmers to sell their produce
directly to private traders or in local markets at prices
which are much higher than the officially offered producer
prices. For instance in the black markets maize can fetch
a price as much as Tsh. 5/= per Kilo and Paddy up to Tsh.
10/= per Kilo.

The system of uniform pan-territorial producer prices for
the whole country was modified with effect from July 1981.
Currently producer prices are differentiated for the areas
depending on the suitability of an area for the specific

crop production. Also consideration is taken of the transport costs of moving the crop from the producing to the consuming area. Prices are set higher in those areas where the growing of particular crops is to be encouraged from the point of view of the overall national objectives. In other areas the government sets a minimum price but the farmers would be free to sell the crop to whoever offers a better price. For example paddy price for the 1981/82 season were fixed at Tsh. 3/= per kg. in Morogoro, Coast, Tanga, Kigoma, Tabora, Mbeya, Mwanza and Shinyanga regions, whereas in the remaining regions the price was set at Tsh. 2/= per kg.[70]

Table 5.12 shows the marketing channels of agricultural crops in the Tanga region.
As already stated above, the cooperative movement in Tanzania was originally created in the context of a capitalist economy. It was expected that the cooperative societies would help to incorporate the peasant producers into the monetary economy. The societies were run by rich peasants who were often elected to leading positions by the peasants on the grounds that they were the most qualified to run these institutions.

Table 5.12: **Marketing Channels for Agricultural Crops in the Tanga Region**

Main crops	Producer sells to/on ...	Produce resold to/on ...
Sisal	Private processor	Exported
Sisal (TSA)	Tanzania Sisal Authority	Exported
Tea	Tanzania Tea Authority	Exported, internal market
Tobacco	Tobacco Authority of Tanzania	Internal processing
Coffee	Coffee Authority of Tanzania	Exported
Cotton	Tanzania Cotton Authority	Exported
Cocoa, Sesam, Sunflower, Cardamom, etc.	GAPEX	Exported
Maize, Sorghum, Rice, Beans, Pulses, Cassava	NMC	Internal marketing
Vegetables, Fruits, etc.	Private traders	Urban markets (mainly)
All food crops	Local markets	Local customers (estate employees)
Coconuts, all food crops	Black markets	Urban markets and in Kenya

Source: Regional Development Director's Office, Tanga

5.2.2.5. The Limitations of the Primary Cooperative Societies

After the Arusha Declaration, the cooperatives gradually became more closely tied to the state and its demands. This intensified the conflict between the notion of the cooperative society as a voluntary association catering primarily for the needs of its members, and of the cooperative society as an agency of change responsive to government demands.
They were unilaterally turned into multi-purpose institutions, although they lacked the managerial capacity to handle all the responsibilities.[71] The limitations of the primary cooperative societies will be illustrated below by the experiences in the Tanga region: the management committees as well as the paid employees lack both experience and business knowledge for the running of the societies. Management problems were reflected in poor accounting. The latter being a very important instrument for monitoring and controlling business. Lack of proper accounting recording made it difficult for one to obtain a full picture of the economic state of societies which were affiliated to the Tanga Cooperative Union;[72] there was poor collection system of the peasants' produce, especially in areas which had a low density of cooperative societies like the Handeni district.

Ideally the societies had an established network of collection points along certain feeder roads. The peasants were supposed to bring their produce of cotton etc. to these points at certain days announced at the beginning of the growing season. A lorry hired by the society was expected to pass and collect the products. The secretary of the society joined the collection tour in order to supervise the weighing and grading of the produce. But the peasants were dissatisfied with the system for a number of reasons:

(a) the collection was often not done according to the time table announced. This was partly due to bad road conditions, breakdown of the vehicles or unreliability of the vehicle contractors. The effects of these occurances were that peasants might have walked for several miles with heavy loads of the produce to be sold, only to find that the lorry was not there. Since storage facilities at the collection points were usually poor or not available, the peasants had to carry their produce back home. In some cases they left the products at the collection point hoping that the lorry might pass on the following days. The result of which was that the products ended up rotting or getting stolen.

(b) another complaint concerning the grading of the produce. The authorities concerned assigned low grades to the products of the peasants and later sold them at higher grades to the Union and pocketed the differences. The societies lost their legitimacy in the eyes of the peasants not only in the Tanga region but the country as a whole.

However, besides the old marketing primary societies for agricultural crops which were abolished because of the weakness pointed in the past section, there are currently three other types of rural cooperative societies in the country. These are the consumer cooperative societies (co-operative shops), savings and credit societies and the generally known as 'other cooperative societies' which include furniture dealers, shoe-makers, saw mills, timber dealers etc. Tables 5.13 and 5.14 show the distribution of these societies in the Korogwe and Handeni districts.

Mombo division in Korogwe district has 60 % of the total number of the village cooperative shops in the district

because it has the largest number of registered villages
(32 %). Korogwe division has the largest number of the
credit and savings societies in the district (50 %) due
to the large number of employees in the sisal estates,
factories and government offices in the district. The district headquarters are located in this division. These
societies are usually initiated by workers who have regular
incomes, hence it is easy to deduct their contributions
from their salaries.
In Handeni district Kwekivu and Mzundu divisions have the
largest number of registered villages but none of them
had a consumer cooperative society. There was only one
consumer society in the whole district at Chanika town,
the district headquarters. Chanika has also three of the
four 'other cooperative societies'. There was no savings
and credit societies in the whole district. The small number of cooperative societies in this district was due to
low cooperative mobilisation in the remote areas.[73]

Cooperative shops had been tried in Tanzania since the
early 1960s when they began with assistance from Israeli.
But the shops were characterised by mismanagement and misappropriation of funds by the office holders. Inspite of
evidence of dishonesty and inefficient management of the
shops in the urban areas, the government decided again
in February 1976 to initiate a mass campaign to start communally owned shops in each village and close down all
private retail shops in the rural areas.[74] Officials in
the regions rushed into closing private shops without even
awaiting policy guidelines from the office of the Prime
Minister.[75]

The effect of this approach was the creation of a great
shortage of goods in the rural areas. President Nyerere
had to intervene and called a stop to the practice of

closing down private shops. The private shop owners who
had lost their trading licences were given back. A rule
was established that no private shop should be closed until
a viable village cooperative shop had been established
and its management proved competent.[76] According to interviews conducted with the cooperative officers in Korogwe
and Handeni districts, the common problems facing the existing village cooperative shops are as follows:
(a) Lack of enough capital to run the shops. Income obtained is not enough to cover the expenses incurred.
(b) Problem of supply of goods due to limited transport
facilities in the remote areas and the current bad
economic situation facing the country as whole which
has resulted to shortages of essential commodities.
Poor communication system leads to lack of information
about the availability of goods at the nearest Regional
Trading Company. For instance a village shop management representative might travel from a remote area
to the RTC branch only to find that there are no supplies of goods. This leads to loss of funds in terms
of fare and also waste of time.
(c) Lack of trained staff with shop management experience
and skills. This leads to loss of funds.

The common problems facing the Savings and Credit Societies
are: lack of trained manpower to run them and educate the
people the significance of them; low savings capacity of
the workers given their low incomes; the membership to
these societies is supposed to be voluntary but in some
work places deductions from the workers' incomes are made
compulsory. A case was experienced in Toronto Sisal Estate
in which workers complained that money was deducted from
their salaries as compulsory, but were not given the opportunity to take credits. Most of the workers thought
the deductions were a kind of insurance which they will

Table 5.13: Distribution of the Existing Cooperative Societies in Korogwe District (Feb. 1983)

Division	Registered Villages	Consumer Coop. Societies	Savings and Credit Societies	Other Coop. Soc.(a)
Korogwe	25	4	3	-
Mombo	37	9	2	-
Bungu	32	2	1	-
Magoma	21	0	0	-
Total	115	15	6	-

(a) = Data for 'Other Cooperative Societies' was not available.
Source: Cooperative Office, Korogwe

Table 5.14: Distribution of the existing Cooperative Societies in Handeni District (Feb. 1983)

Division	Registered Villages	Consumer Coop. Societies	Savings and Credit Societies	Other Coop. Soc.
Chanika	8	1	-	3
Magamba	12	-	-	-
Sindeni	11	-	-	-
Mgera	9	-	-	-
Mswaki	9	-	-	-
Kwamsisi	6	-	-	-
Kwekivu	13	-	-	-
Mzundu	13	-	-	1
Mazingara	6	-	-	-

Kimbe	7	-	-	-
Mkumburu	8	-	-	-
Total	102	1	-	4

Source: Cooperative Office, Handeni

get back when they stopped working. But those who have left work have experienced difficulties in getting their money. As a result of frequent transfers of the managers and lack of proper records, the new management claimed not to be informed of the past activities.[77]

The 'other village cooperative societies' had the following limitations: there was the difficulty of raw material supply. When they are available were very expensive; there was theft of the product in the field in the case of timber dealers. The latter also face the problem of transport; there was lack of working instruments for furniture dealers, timber-cutters, shoe-makers, miners etc.; problem of marketing the final products. For example shoe-makers had to compete with advanced producers like the BORA Shoes Company. One solution to this could be to improve their skills and quality of the products to make them more competitive; the leadership of the societies was still poor and sometimes dishonest. Some of the leaders took the product to sell to distant markets and pocketed part of the income. This discouraged the other members.

In order to help the cooperative societies in the rural areas to reduce the problem of management including bookkeeping, the government in collaboration with the Tanga Integrated Rural Development Programme have started a Village Shop Management Training Programme for the village functionaries whose activities touch the development of the cooperative shops. These include the shop-keepers, village secretaries and members of the village shop-committees. The training is financed by the TIRDEP but the residence and transport costs for the participants are paid by the Prime Minister's Office. The course is a five weeks programme composed of three phases, i.e. classroom seminar, follow-up on the job-training and a residential evaluation at the training centre.[78]

5.2.2.6. Agricultural Extension and Other Rural Socio-Economic Services

The new villages did not manage to solve the problem of government's efforts to reach the peasants and mobilize them to increase agricultural production. This has been reflected by the performance and distribution of extension services. Their effectiveness on peasant agricultural production declined to the extent that in 1976 President Nyerere himself claimed in a public speech that Tanzanian agriculture would do as well without the extension services. The latter was characterised by the following obstacles:
(a) there was a high average number of peasant farmers per extension worker. For example in 1979 the number of farmers per extension worker in the Tanga region was: Korogwe (1200), Muheza (800), Handeni (600), Lushoto (600) and Pangani (200) The average number for the region was 700 farmers per extension worker.
In order to ease the problem of extension service in the rural areas in the region, the regional authorities together with the TIRDEP have started in March 1982 a programme called 'Training and Visiting System' in which groups of farmers (40) are selected by the Village Council and undergo intensive training on 'modern'

methods of agricultural production. The knowledge acquired is expected to be passed to other peasants in the villages. The number of 'contacted' farmers will increase with availability of extension service facilities. The content of training depends on the ecological conditions of the area.

The limitations facing this programme are: the selection of the farmers could be doubtful because they might not be the best; the project is too expensive, especially in terms of follow-up expenses which include transport facilities. It is doubtful whether the local authorities will be able to meet the expenses when the Germans hand-over the whole programme; the training extension workers are not enough at the moment. There is one for each ward and sometimes are used including the vehicles by the district authorities for political activities, hence have no enough time for their original duties.[79]

(b) As a result of the present government strong need for foreign exchange, a great part of the extension work is still devoted to export-crop production, especially cotton in the case of the Korogwe and Handeni districts. Extension service for food production is relatively neglected. This is a contradiction to the government policy which emphasizes on food production.

(c) The poor living and working conditions of the extension workers reduce their effectiveness. Most of them work in the remote areas, transport and other communication facilities are very poor. Some of the peasant farmers do not even know of the existence of extension services. This is because they have no contact with them, particularly in those areas where no export crops are grown.

In 1979 about 19 % of the total length of the roads in the region were within the Korogwe district. Handeni district had only 6.1 %. Moreover, Korogwe had 40 % of the total length of the railway lines in the region. Handeni had none. The main weakness of the existing communication system in the rural areas of the region is the poor state of the feeder roads. This is more true in Handeni. Currently the TIRDEP and the regional authorities have started a programme to rehabilitate the deteriorated roads in the district.

In May 1977 the government directed that all technical field staff in the wards should for sometime live in the villages. They were to live on night allowances paid by the government. This was to avoid their being a financial burden to the villagers. Later the government faced the problem of lack of funds to pay the night allowances and vehicles to ensure the transport of the staff. Based on these limitations the government decided in 1978 to post officials on a permanent basis to 4,000 of the country's 8,000 villages. The aspect of night allowances was removed. The new village officials were named 'village managers'. They were to be general managers of the village affairs under the Village Council. Their role became ambiguous as they came into conflict with the village Party leadership who dominated all the political and socio-economic affairs of the villages.[80]

5.2.2.5.1. Education Facilities

The access to education facilities is of utmost importance for the creation of a basis for future socio-economic development. In November 1977, Tanzania started her policy

of Universal Primary Education for all children who have reached the school age (7 to 8 years). By the end of the year more than 900,000 children were registered to start primary education.
The rapid extension of primary education for a poor country like Tanzania has posed problems of insufficient teaching material, qualified teachers and other school facilities.

A research project on 'The Falling of Educational Standards in Primary Schools in Tanzania' which was conducted by a group of Education Students of the University of Dar es salaam, showed that the common problems in the primary schools visited by the group were lack of text-books, science apparatus, furniture such as desks and chairs etc. The training of teachers and the living and working conditions of the graduate teachers also contribute much to the quality of education provided to the children.[81]

For instance, in order to meet the acute shortage of teachers for the programme, the training period of the teachers (Grade C) has been reduced from two years to one year. Moreover, the Colleges of National Education are so much involved in "Self-reliance" activities particularly agricultural work that the period of effective total academic course could be two to three months only. The course is so crushed a programme that the teachers coming out of these colleges are not well qualified.
Table 5.15 shows the relationship between Primary Schools, classrooms and teachers' houses in the district of the Tanga region.
Table 5.15 indicates that the average number of pupils per classroom in the region at the end of 1982 was 55. Muheza district had the highest number of pupils per classroom (76). The normal standard of pupils per classroom in the region was 45.

Table 5.15: Distribution of Primary Schools, Classrooms and Teachers' Houses in the Tanga Region (1982)

Districts	Schools	Number of Classrooms	Teachers	Classrooms per School	Pupils per Classroom	Number of Teachers	Pupils per Teacher
Handeni	130	469	111	3.6	54	528	45
Korogwe	138	544	177	3.9	54	1,027	39
Lushoto	158	663	200	4.2	54	1,195	48
Muheza	135	370	229	2.7	76	1,188	41
Pangani	30	94	25	3.1	49	94	35
Tanga	41	330	-	8.0	36	415	40
Region	632	2,470	742	3.9	55	4,447	43

Source: Regional Education Office, Tanga

According to the Regional Education Officer, 25 % of the
2470 classrooms shown on Table 5.15 were housed in temporary buildings which were poorly furnished and sometimes
there was no classroom equipment at all. The children have
to sit on the floor. It is not uncommon to see 5 to 7 pupils or more in a classroom sharing a single text book.
The situation becomes more serious when it comes to general
science classes where due to lack of apparatuses pupils
have just to watch an experiment performed by the teacher.
Moreover, Table 5.15 shows that at the end of 1982 the
regional average number of pupils per teacher was 43. Lushoto and Handeni districts had figures above the average.

As far as teachers houses are concerned, there were more
teachers than houses available. As a result of the shortage
of houses many of the newly appointed teachers to the rural
areas have to find some accomodation with the village people.
Most of this accomodation is not conducive for the proper
preparation of lessons. For instance there is no adequate
light or furniture.

As far as Secondary Education is concerned, all the day
Secondary Schools in the region are located in the Tanga
town. Consequently, there is a higher chance for standard
seven school leavers living in Tanga town to be selected
for secondary education than for pupils from other districts of the region. This is due to accomodation expenses.
The children in Tanga town can stay at home. It is well
known at the Regional Education Office in Tanga that parents
like to bring their children to Tanga town when they enter
standard seven in order to give them a better chance for
the selection to secondary education.[82]

For the past ten years an average of 19.2 % of the standard seven leavers have been selected for secondary education from Tanga town primary schools but the figure for the other districts was 8.7 %.

On New Year's Eve, 31st December, 1969, President Nyerere addressed the nation over the radio on the theme of Adult Education. He declared 1970 as "Adult Education Year". The speech constituted a great landmark in the history of adult education in Tanzania. It explained to the people the nature, scope and philosophy of adult education. It urged the entire nation to embark on massive adult education programmes. The importance of adult education for both the country and every individual citizen was emphasized on the fact that the country is poor and the majority of the people especially in the rural areas are pessimistic and accept their existing conditions as the "Will of God".[83]

Therefore, the first objective of adult education is to shake the people out of this resignation. This is similar to what Paulo Freiere referred to as a process of "conscientization" in which he argued the need for changing the adult's pessimism and fatalistic perspective of reality and enabling him to acquire a "critical" vision of his environment and an awareness of his capacity to change his environment.[84]

Amid the vague notion which the majority of the people had about the meaning of adult education, Nyerere defined it as "learning anything which can help the masses of the people to understand the environment they live in and the manner in which they can change it and use it to improve their own conditions. People have to learn how to produce more on their farms or in their factories and offices. They have to learn about better food and what a blanced diet is and how it can be obtained by their own efforts. He further argued that the above was only possible if all

members of the nation worked together for their common
good. This means that adult education should also help
the people to understand the national policies of socialism and self-reliance.[85]

Adult education was to be related to a number of activities
in the rural areas, e.g. farmers' education programmes
led by the regional agricultural staff, small-scale industries programmes run by regional industrial staff, national
service cottage industries programmes run by the National
Service; public health and nutrition campaigns led by the
medical staff. All the above activities were to be integrated and related to each other through the help of special
radio programmes. In the Tanga region, the activities of
adult education are largely confined to functional literacy classes and some rural library services. Table 5.16
shows the enrolment of adult education in the region till
1980.

There are some differences in respect to the adult education
programmes between the districts. Pangani and Handeni had
the highest enrolment in relation to the total size of
the population. This is because the two districts are the
ones with the highest rate of illiteracy in the region.
Korogwe, Lushoto and Muheza are roughly in the similar
middle position while Tanga with a much higher average
level of education in the town has the largest enrolment.
It is difficult to say how many people are enrolled in
the several consecutive years and how many are newly enrolled in a particular year because a substantial part
of the enrolment in different years actually consists of
the same people. Moreover, genuine attendance in adult
education classes is lower than the given figure.
Less than 20 % of all adult education teachers are professional teachers. The majority are volunteers drawn from
a wide range of different professions.

Table 5.16: Enrolment of Adult Education in the
Tanga Region (1980)

District	Functional Literacy Classes	Registered Enrolment	% of Total Population	Participants per Class
Handeni	652	29,340	15.9	45
Korogwe	713	18,538	9.7	26
Lushoto	1,463	30,723	10.7	21
Pangani	263	6,838	10.5	26
Tanga	175	5,075	3.5	29
Muheza	893	21,432	10.7	24
Region	4,132	111,564	10.2	27

Source: Regional Education Office, Tanga

However, there are several factors which have made it difficult to achieve the ambitious goals of adult education programme as already stated above. The following are some of the most important obstacles:

First, the voluntary teaching staff has usually good intentions, but is often not sufficiently qualified for teaching functional adult education.

Second, usually the money allocated for adult education activities arrive so late in the year that material cannot be bought in time.

Third, experimental fields used for functional agricultural training are not adequate and materials like seeds, fertilizer etc. are not easily available and when available are very expensive.

Fourth, some of the classes opened had to be closed because people were shifting to different places in search of food or in response to other socio-economic pressures such as employment possibilities, new settlement schemes etc.

Fifth, transport for adult education supervisors in the divisions and wards is a great problem. Most of them do not have bicycles, motor cycles or other means of transport. Sixth, there is need for a stronger organisational foundation and more support from administrative and political circles for important adult education activities like radio lessons, correspondance courses, workers' education and upgrading of teachers.

5.2.2.6.1. **Health Facilities**

For a country like Tanzania where the majority of the population lives in the countryside, the development of health facilities for the rural masses is an important aspect of socio-economic development. This is because of the simple fact that it is only healthy people who can work effectively.
Only about 7 % of the total population of the Tanga region do not live within 10 kms of any stationary health facility compared to the national average of 22 %.[86]
However, there is unequal distribution of the health facilities in the region. This is supported by Table 5.17 which shows a comparison of the distribution of these facilities in the Korogwe and Handeni districts. As a result of the existence of many sisal estates Korogwe has more health facilities than Handeni.
Moreover, the Table shows that the dispensary is the basis of medical service in the region. 28.2 % of the total number of government dispensaries and 26.7 % of those owned by the sisal estates in the region are located in Korogwe district. Handeni has only 17 % of the government dispensaries and 2 dispensaries run by the estates. But it has 50 % of the total number of the hospitals run by non-government agencies in the region.

Table 5.17: Comparative Distribution of Health Facilities between Korogwe and Handeni District (1979)

District	Dispensaries Govt.	Non-Govt.(a) Agencies	Sisal Est.	Hospitals Govt.	Non-Govt.(a)	Health Centers	% of Population within 10 km of health facilities
Handeni	17	8	2	1	-	3	10.1
Korogwe	29	-	16	1	1	2	36.5
Total Region	103	16	60	6	4	12	23.0

(a) = Most of the Non-Government Agencies are Missionary Organisations

Source: Regional Development Director's Office, Tanga

There is only one hospital in the Handeni district run by the government at Chanika.
However, most of the existing health facilities in the region such as buildings, equipment etc. are in very poor conditions and need great improvement if at all they are to serve the people effectively. There is a need for better and qualified staff. Regular supervision and professional advice to dispensary staff originating from the big hospitals and rural Health Centres remain difficult and insufficient because of poor transport and communication systems and the heavy work load at the centres themselves.[87]

5.2.2.6.2. Water Supply

Availability of rural water supply is another important element for a better quality life of the rural population. In the rural areas water has different uses: for domestic

use, cattle watering, irrigation etc. In this section we
shall deal with water for domestic uses.

Before independence most of the water supply development
was concentrated in towns estates, minor settlements and
trading centres. These were mostly administrative locations
where European officials were stationed. There were a few
water supplies constructed by the Department of Agriculture
for local cattle watering in the rural areas.[88]

The Tanzania government has set a goal of providing adequate water supplies for its entire rural population within
a period of 20 years since 1970. The programme started
with the launching of the Second Five Year Development
Plan (1969-1974). This is an enormous undertaking in a
vast country which presently has about 20 million people.
The improvement of water services ranges from large storage
dams with kilometers of distribution piping shallow seepage
holes dug in a dry stream bad. According to the government
'adequate water' means that the source of water is protected from the more gross forms of pollution; and that people
expend less effort to obtain the water than from other
traditional sources and that no better supply can be developed for the same level of expenditure. Therefore emphasis is still on communal stand-pipes. These are either pumped
or flow by gravity schemes. Adequate water for the rural
people is also provided by handdug wells in the sparsely
populated areas with seasonal stream flow and a high groundwater table.[89]

The following types of water supplies according to the
type of water source exist in the region: surface water
which include rivers and streams (supply is by pumping
or by gravity). This is common in Korogwe and Lushoto districts; dams where rain water collects in a blocked valley

or water basin. This is common in Handeni and Muheza districts; groundwater sources such as wells where supply is by lifting the water with a bucket, a hand-pump or a motor-driven pump. These are common throughout the region; boreholes where water is lifted with pumps.

In 1979 about 6 million people in the whole country had access to water supplies. Tanga region had 10 % of the total number. This was about 30 % of the regional population. This does not mean that two third of the population in the region had no water supply. But often the water is not clean and might be far away from the place of living, so that a lot of time is spent on fetching water from a distant source.

The districts which are relatively well served are those with large number of estates such as Korogwe, Muheza and Pangani. In 1979 about 31 % of the population of Korogwe had adequate water supply. The figure for Handeni was only 12 %.[90]

The Handeni Trunk Main Project (Water project) which started in 1974 is expected to supply half of the population of the district with drinking water. Currently 55 villages are already served by the project. The water is drawn from the Pangani river near Korogwe town.
However, for the Regional Planners the future attention should be on how to help the villagers especially in the Handeni district with water for irrigation. This is because presently little consideration has been done on how rural water development will affect agricultural production including animal husbandry. Frequently this aspect is unspecified and its occurance is assumed to be automatic.
In addition to above, most of the government moves in the area of rural water development have in practice involved

little local initiative in the planning of projects and
there is little local contribution to the implementation
process. The government plans, builds, operates and maintains the projects. The labour force is fully paid and
the water is free for the consumers. This is contrary to
the national policy of self-reliance. The Regional Water
Engineer claimed that self-help is inefficient and not
dependable, hence it cannot be integrated well into a tight
construction schedule. But the question to be asked is
how can local responsibility towards a water supply scheme
be fostered if complete ownership and control remains outside the community served, especially given the current
limited financial resources in the country?
There is ample experience throughout the region and the
country at large to show that self-help labour can be
successful in rural water projects.[91]

5.3. Summary

Chapter five examined the relationships between the government and the peasants in Tanzania, especially in the Tanga
region. The purpose was to investigate their response to
the government's efforts to make them increase agricultural
production.

The investigation started by introducing some of the theories concerning the characteristics of the peasants in
Africa. Some of these theories argue that the African peasantry as a class is a colonial creation and is still in
the making. They all agree that the largest part of the
peasantry in Africa is still marginally integrated in the
monetary economy and that the efforts of the governments
to make them respond to their demands to increase agricultural production have generally not yet been successful.

The theories were then examined in relation to the experiences of the Tanga region and Tanzania at large. The following aspects were analysed:

(i) The background to peasant export-production in the region. It was seen that peasant production for export in the Tanga region did not begin with colonialism. There was already production for export to Zanzibar in the region before colonial establishment. The commodities which were exported include butter, cattle, goats, sorghum, coconuts, slaves etc. The most important ports were Tanga and Pangani. Colonialism integrated the regional economy more in the world market by introducing new export-crops like coffee, cotton and tea including new production methods which have been regarded by the peasants as too demanding.

(ii) The colonial agriculture and its demands were inherited by the post independence government. In order to make the peasants increase production, the government started with two different approaches to rural development, i.e. the transformation and improvement approach. The former aimed at increasing peasant agricultural production through the establishment of government supervised settlement schemes. Peasants from areas with land shortage like the Usambaras were taken to new areas where it was hoped that they would be more open to change. The settlements failed due to overcapitalisation, i.e. there was more machinery than necessary in relation to land and labour available. Moreover, tension between the 'settlers' and the government supervisors was quite common. The former felt that they were not free to do things as they wanted. The settlements were also heavily indebted.

The improvement approach was based on training the

peasants in their traditional environments on 'modern' methods of agricultural production through the establishment of Farmers' Training Centres and by providing extension services to the interested farmers (progressive farmers). This led to social differentiation in the rural areas.

(iii) As a result of the failures of the past approaches and the development of social differentiations in the rural areas, the Party and government redefined the rural development policy in 1967 through the Arusha Declaration. Its two fundamental principles were 'self-reliance and socialism'. The former meant peasants' implementation of rural development projects without depending on aid from outside. Socialism meant absence of exploitation, corruption and social differentiation in society.

The most important part of the new approach was the creation of communal villages based on traditional African values called 'Ujamaa' villages. Theoretically the villages were to be established voluntarily by convinced peasants. Nevertheless the 'Ujamaa' programme was characterised by ideological ambiguity and technological limitations. The work of convincing the peasants on the advantages of 'socialism' was entrusted to administrators and field officers who had been previously in charge of implementation of colonial policies. The peasants reacted to the policy with a set of attitudes that ranged from scepticism and mistrust to outright resentment. This led to slow development of the villagization programme. Moreover, by stressing the primacy of the hoe cultivation in the villages, the policy left the productive forces untouched. Hence it failed to improve productivity in agriculture, especially in communal farms. This was intensified by the drought of 1973 which greatly reduced grain production in the country. The government announced compulsory villagization by 1975. Force was to be used. Peasant agricultural production had to be increased at any cost. The form of production, i.e. whether communal or private became of secondary significance. The government also decided to abolish all the primary cooperative societies which were responsible for the marketing of peasant produce. These were characterised by mismanagement and corruption.

The current Crop Authorities have also been found to be unreliable and concentrate their services including input supplies on export crops. Food crops are almost neglected.

Other rural cooperative societies include consumer societies, savings and credit societies formed in work places and the generally known as 'other cooperatives' like for timber dealers, shoe makers, miners etc. The common problems facing these societies are lack of capital, supply of goods, transport and poor management.
Lastly, the Chapter examined the distribution of rural socio-economic services such as agricultural extension, education, health and water for domestic purposes. It was seen that there is unequal distribution of these facilities in the different parts of the region. They are mostly concentrated in those areas where there is export-production. The colonial legacy of unequal development of socio-economic infrastructure has not yet been solved.

Footnotes for Chapter five

1. Teodor Shanin, *Peasants and Peasant Societies*, Penguin Books 1971, p. 16.

2. Goran Hyden, *Beyond Ujamaa in Tanzania*, Berkeley: University of California Press 1980, pp. 1-18.

3. See Samir Amin, *Capitalism and Ground Rent: The Domination of Capitalism over Agriculture in Tropical Africa*, Dakar, DEP, 1974, and also see Mahmood Mamdani, *Politics and Class Formation in Uganda*, New York, Monthly Review Press, 1976.

4. J. C. de Wilde, *Experiences with Agricultural Development in Tropical Africa*, Vol. I, John Hopkins Press, Baltimore 1976, pp. 21-22.

5. John Saul and Roger Woods, *African Peasantries*, in Dennis L. Cohen (ed.), *Political Economy of Africa*, Longman 1981, p. 113.

6. Eric Wolf, *Peasants*, New Jersey, Prentice Hill, 1966, p. 20.

7. Marilyn Silberfein, *The African Cultivator: A Geographical Overview*, Crossroads Press 1978, p. 8.

8. Philip W. Porter, *Climate and Agriculture in Africa*, in C. G. Knight (ed.), *Contemporary Africa, Geography and Change*, New Jersey, Prentice Hill, 1976, pp. 112-39.

9. Matthias U. Igboruzike, *Ecological Balance in Tropical Africa*, Berkeley: University of California Press, 1963, p. 24.

10. FAO, *Production Yearbook*, Vol. 25, Rome 1971 and 1973, Tables 136-38.

11. D. K. Leonard, *Reaching the Peasant Farmer*, Chicago 1977, p. 245.

12. Francis Hill, *Experiments with a Public Sector - Peasantry: Agricultural Schemes and Class Formation in Africa*, Boston 1976.

13. V. Harlow, *History of East Africa*, Vol. II, Oxford University Press 1973, p. 19.

14. Oskar Baumann, *Usambara und seine Nachbargebiete*, Berlin 1891.

15. Karl Garrger, Tangaland und die Kolonisation Deutsch-Ostafrika, Berlin 1898, pp. 16-18.

16. RKA, Nr. 120, Bl. 107.

17. Ibid., Bl. 109.

18. TIRDEP, Tanga Regional Development Plan 1975-1980, Tanga, TIRDEP, 1975, p. 52.

19. See J. Illife, Tanzania under German Rule, DSM 1975, p. 68, and also see B. D. Bowles The Political Economy of Colonial Tanganyika, DSM, 1974, p. 10.

20. International Bank of Reconstruction and Development, The Economic Development of Tanganyika, Baltimore, Johns Hopkins Press, 1961, p. 129.

21. Goran Hyden, op. cit., p. 72.

22. Government of Tanganyika, People's Plan, DSM, 1962, also see Goran Hyden, op. cit., p. 72.

23. M. Yeager, Limitations of the Early Post-Independence Village Settlement Schemes, DSM, 1972.

24. H. Newiger, Evaluation of the Villagization Policies in Tanzania (DSM, Mimeo), 1968.

25. Goran Hyden, op. cit., p. 73.

26. I. Bavu, Leadership and Communication in the Ujamaa Process: A Case Study of Kabuku-Ndani Ujamaa Village Cooperative Society, Unpublished.

27. René Dumont, Tanzania Agriculture after the Arusha Declaration, DSM, Government Printer, 1969, p. 8.

28. Clyde Ingle, From Village to State in Tanzania, The Politics of Rural Development, Ithaca, Cornell University Press, 1972, p. 51.

29. R. W. Kates and J. Mckay, Twelve new Settlements in Tanzania, BRALUP, UDSM, 1969.

30. Poul Westergaard, Farm Surveys of Cashew Producers in Mtwara Region, ERB, Paper 68, 3, UDSM, 1968, p. 8.

31. J. Liebenow, Colonial Rule and Political Development in Tanzania: The Case of the Makonde, Evanston, North-Western University Press, 1971, pp. 296-300.

32. H. U. E. Thoden van Velzen, Staff Kulaks and Peasants, in Cliffe and Saul, Socialism in Tanzania, Vol. 2, Nairobi, EAPH, 1974, pp. 153-79.

33. J. H. Kouter, Facts and Factors in Rural Economy of the Nyakyusa in Tanzania (mimeo), Afrika Studienzentrum, Leiden 1974.

34. J. K. Nyerere, Socialism and Rural Development, in J. K. Nyerere, Freedom and Development, Oxford University Press, pp. 6-14.

35. G. Hyden (1980), op. cit., p. 113.

36. J. K. Nyerere, op. cit., p. 8.

37. I. Batu, op. cit., p. 17.

38. Operation Dodoma was a government-planned programme to move all the people in the Dodoma Region into villages with the hope of developing these villages into communal places of life and work and to convince them, the President spent a long time living in one of the first villages to be set up in the area called Chamwino.

39. TIRDEP, op. cit., pp. 48-49.

40. Henry Mapolu and Gerard Philipson, Agricultural Co-operation and Development of the Productive Forces: Some Lessons from Tanzania, Africa Development, Dakar, Vol. I, No. 1 (1976), p. 32.

41. Goran Hyden (1980), op. cit., p. 121.

42. F. M. Lofchie, Agrarian Crisis and Economic Liberalism in Tanzania, Los Angeles 1975, p. 16, also see D. E. MacHenry (Jr.), Policy Implementation in Rural Tanzania - The Ujamaa Villages, DSM, 1975, p. 19, and see Goran Hyden, op. cit., p. 130.

43. D. E. MacHenry (Jr.), op. cit., p. 19.

44. I. Kopytoff, Socialism and Traditional African Societies, in African Socialism 1975, p. 54.

45. G. Macpherson, Village Technology for Rural Development, Agricultural Innovation in Tanzania, DSM, 1976, pp. 23-24.

46. H. Mapolu (1976), op. cit., p. 34.

47. Election Study Committee, Socialism and Participation, DSM, Tanzania Publishing House, 1975.

48. Interview with the Handeni District Chairman, Ndugu H. Majili.

49. TIRDEP, op. cit., p. 59.

50. Goran Hyden (1980), op. cit., p. 130.

51. J. K. Nyerere, The Arusha Declaration. Ten Years After, DSM, Government Printer, 1977, p. 41.

52. Interview with Cooperative Officer, Handeni, also see TIRDEP, op. cit., p. 60.

53. Interview with Ndugu H. Majili, op. cit.

54. GTZ, Lower Mkomazi Irrigation Project, Tanzania, Main Report, Eschborn 1982, p. 21.

55. Daily News, 20th October, 1974, p. 1.

56. Marketing Development Bureau, Ministry of Agriculture, Large-scale Maize Production, DSM, Dec. 1976.

57. Interview with the Cooperative Officers, Handeni and Korogwe.

58. Goran Hyden (1980), op. cit., p. 24.

59. D. Leonard, op. cit., p. 245.

60. Interview with the Regional Development Agricultural Officer, Tanga.

61. Block farming is the term using when a sizeable area is cultivated for particular common crops but each family maintains responsibility for the cultivation and proceeds of its block.

62. United Republic of Tanzania, The Villages and Ujamaa Villages, Registration, Designation and Administration Act, 1975, Government Notice No. 162 (22nd August, 1975).

63. F. M. Lofchie, op. cit., p. 6, also see D. E. MacHenry (Jr.), op. cit., p. 22.

64. Cooperative Development Division, Notes on the Cooperative Movement in Tanzania, DSM, Ministry of Agriculture, 1975, p. 2.

65. Goran Haden, Efficiency Versus Distribution in East African Cooperatives, Nairobi, EALB, 1964, p. 3.

66. William H. Friedland, African Socialism, Stanford University Press 1964, p. 24.

67. Kurt B. Anschel-Russel, Agricultural Cooperatives and Markets in Developing Countries, New York 1969, p. 313-326.

68. G. K. Heilleiner, Agricultural Marketing in Tanzania, Policies and Problems, ERB, Paper 68.11, DSM, 1970, pp. 4-7.

69. Wolfgang Schneider-Barthold, Farmers' Reaction to the Present Economic Situation in Tanzania: A Case Study of Five Villages in the Kilimanjaro Region, GDI, 1983, p. 16.

70. GTZ, op. cit., p. 27.

71. Goran Hyden (1980), op. cit., p. 133.

72. TIRDEP, op. cit., p. 115-16.

73. Interview with the Cooperative Officers, Korogwe and Handeni.

74. Goran Hyden (1980), op. cit., p. 132.

75. Daily News, DSM, 20th February, 1976, p. 1.

76. Daily News, DSM, 24th March, 1976, p. 1.

77. Interview with the randomly selected workers in the surveyed sisal plantations.

78. Interview with the Cooperative Officers, Korogwe and Handeni.

79. Interview with one of the TIRDEP Extension Training Officers, Korogwe.

80. Interview with the District Development Director, Korogwe, Ndugu Babu, and the District Planning Officer, Handeni.

81. R. Mathias, The Falling of Educational Standards in Primary Schools in Tanzania, Dept. of Education, UDSM, 1977 (Unpublished), p. 3.

82. Interview with the Regional Education Officer, Tanga.

83. J. K. Nyerere, New Year Speech on Adult Education, DSM, 31st Dec. 1969.

84. Paulo Freire, Padagogy of the Oppressed, Herder & Herder, 1970.

85. J. K. Nyerere, Adult Education Year, in Freedom and Development, Oxford University Press.

86. Interview with the Regional Medical Officer, Tanga.

87. TIRDEP, op. cit., p. 249.

88. D. Warner, Formulating Guidelines for Rural Water Investment: The Case Study of Tanzania, DSM, 1976.

89. United Republic of Tanzania, Second Five Year Plan for Economic and Social Development, 1st July, 1969-70, July 1974, Vol. I, DSM, Government Printer, 1969.

90. Water Development Office, Tanga.

91. D. Warner, op. cit., p. 5.

VI. CONCLUSIONS

6.1. Proletarianization of the Peasantry

A historical and empirical investigation of the response of the local peasantry in the Tanga region to wage labour in the sisal plantations has shown that even the present sisal plantation system has failed to bring about the proletarianization of the peasantry. The plantations have only been able to attract a migrant type of labour. This is because of the poor working and living conditions. The wages are low, housing facilities are poor and there is insecurity of employment. Demand for labour fluctuates with prices of the sisal product on the world market. Moreover, there is no old age social security. Therefore, the labourers have to maintain links with their areas of origin.

The failure of the plantations to proletarianize the peasantry has the following long term effects:
(i) the migrant nature of the labourers has led to the perpetuation of the unskilled labour character of the labour force in the region and the country as a whole.
(ii) the above mentioned factor impedes innovation in the labourers' places of origin, especially for those labourers from outside the region.

Efforts to improve the working and living conditions of the labourers in the plantations are limited by poor management and financial resources. The latter is due to the present economic crisis facing the country. This is true for those state owned plantations.

The author would like to suggest that the existing areas of the sisal plantations could be reduced to march with the available management and financial capacity. Moreover, given the fluctuating demand for sisal on the world market and the present food shortages in the region and Tanzania as a whole, it is advisable for the government to increase the diversification of production from sisal to food crops. This could help save the large amounts of foreign exchange used to import food.

6.2. Rural Development Programmes

The other aspect examined in the study was the relationship between the peasants and the government in the region. It was seen that since the colonial establishment in the region the peasants have reacted to socio-economic changes initiated by the government with a mixture of apathy and open resistance. For example, in the Handeni district the peasants have openly resisted the cultivation of cotton and 'Ujamaa' development programmes. They view these programmes as more in the interests of the government rather than themselves.

As a result of this hidden and sometimes open-resistance by the peasants the use of coercion has been one of the major features of rural development in the Tanga region.

It is therefore, suggested that:
(i) in areas where coercion has always been applied to bring about socio-economic changes efforts could be made to establish a new relationship between the government and the peasantry. This is because as long as there is no trust between the two, all development programmes made by the government in the rural areas including financial inputs will not have any lasting positive impact.

(ii) only feasible promises could be made to the peasants, i.e. those which have a realistic chance of implementation. This would enable the advices of dedicated skilled staff in the rural areas to be more accepted.
(iii) as far as the developing of a spirit of self-reliance among the peasantry is concerned, the poor peasants should not only be objects of crop regulations and other orders from the government, and victims of the influence of rich peasants. Serious efforts should be made by the government to find ways of involving them directly in the development policies.

6.2.1. Distribution of Agricultural Extension Services

In order to have an economic utilisation of agricultural services like credits, input supplies, cultivation assistance etc. in the rural areas the following factors could be taken into consideration:

(i) preferance could be given to those villagers who are prepared to bear the costs of a service rather than those who want it free of charge;
(ii) the services could be provided to productive purposes out of which its costs could be recovered. This implies that the 'Ujamaa villages' could be made cost conscious and realise that investment funds have to be preserved and to be repaid after a certain period. This is because socialist development is also based on careful utilization of scarce resources. The new villages should not be like those of the settlement programmes in the 1960s which proved to be expensive and unproductive.
(iii) whereever possible maximum use could be made of the self-help labour contributions of the people directly benefiting from a particular project. Foreign

aid should only come when there is really need for it.

The Tanga region and Tanzania as a whole are facing serious food shortages because of low productivity. This is because of the fact that agricultural extension services are mostly concentrated on export crop production. Greater priority should now be given to the improvement of food production.
The living and working conditions of the agricultural extension staff including salaries, transport and housing should be improved to encourage them to render their services in the rural areas instead of staying at the headquarters or research centres where they are mostly underutilized.

The distribution of other socio-economic services like education, health, transport and water supplies show that the colonial legacy has not yet been resolved. Most of these services are still concentrated in the export crop production areas. However, even in the latter areas the existing services are in very poor condition as will be shown below:

6.2.2. Education Services

As far as education services are concerned, the author would like to emphasize the following:
(i)   the major objective in primary education which is the basis of education in the country, should be improvement in quality and efficiency rather than the expansion of number of schools. The purpose should be to raise the enrolment ratio by increasing the number of pupils who complete the fully primary

cycle instead of augmenting the number of pupils in the entering grades.

(ii) it is essential that teachers of higher quality, with at least secondary education, are employed and a major effort made to develop an 'appropriate rural educational technology' which includes appropriate textbooks, visual aids, the use of radio and other teaching aids. This would provide a solid foundation for the subsequent extension of primary education to the entire school-age population. Attractive and expensive school buildings, though desirable, are not necessary. The local villagers should be required to construct the school buildings with local labour and materials, thus allowing the government to concentrate its resources on teachers, texts and other essential equipment.

(iii) the improvement of teachers' working and living conditions should be taken as part of improving the quality of primary education. Teachers need proper housing if they are expected to be efficient in the execution of their duties.

In the case of adult education, there is need for better coordination between all the institutions responsible at national, regional and district level to find ways of providing the necessary material for adult education in the rural areas.

6.2.3. Health and Water Facilities

It was observed that the dispensary was the basis of medical services in the rural areas of the region. But the existing dispensaries require great improvement in terms of facilities and more qualified staff. Regular supervision and professional advice from the big hospitals could be given maximum consideration.

More emphasis could be on preventive medical services. There is still a heavy bias on curative medicine despite the Party policy of "Health Campaigns". The significance of preventive medical services lies on the fact that in the long run the health care of the rural people will depend on their own commitment. This implies that emphasis should not only be on improvement of facilities which are normally expensive but on health services within a reasonable reach, which do not only care for immediate and common diseases but which can also help them to prevent the recurrence of diseases and at the same time raise their health and nutritional position.

As far as water supply facilities are concerned, given the present limited financial resources, there is need to foster local responsibility towards the ownership and maintenance of rural water supplies. Currently the ownership and control remains outside the community served.

Moreover, most of the suggested socio-economic changes should contribute to the liberation of the rural women in the region and Tanzania at large. This is because currently it is the women in the rural areas who have to fetch water from distant places, carry sick children to distant dispensaries, carry goods on their heads to distant markets and who for a long time have been denied the opportunity of formal education. Moreover, taking into consideration that food crop production in the rural areas is still the responsibility of women, shows the significant role which women play in the survival of the nation as a whole.

Therefore, any solution to the problem of insufficient food production has to be based on full participation of the women in the rural areas.

6.3. Lessons Derived from the Findings

(i) The poor living and working conditions of the wage-labourers in the sisal plantations surveyed suggests that it is not justifiable to generalize the concept of 'labour aristocracy' to the whole working class in Africa. The wage earners are not better off than the peasantry. In fact most of them are migrant workers who continue to maintain their relations with their places of origin in the rural areas because their places of employment do not offer them old age social security. There is also insecurity of employment.

(ii) The notion of 'political conservatism' attributed to the working class in Africa is also not justifiable. The study has shown that despite the limitations of workers' participation in the management of their places of employment, the workers in the sisal plantations and other areas of employment in Tanzania have since the colonial period struggled in different forms against the oppression of their employers and for better conditions of work. However, as a result of low education and their migrant character they have not been able to form a trade union of their own.

(iii) The Argument that the peasants in Africa are independent of other social classes is also unjustifiable. The study of peasants in the Tanga region and Tanzania

at large has shown that although the peasant owns
his means of production and is self-employed, he
is subjected to exploitation and is a victim of socio-economic policies from outside his own community,
especially from the state. In Tanzania and Africa
as a whole, much of the exploitation of the peasantry
is not done by individual capitalists, but by the
state acting as entrepreneur. The state induces the
peasants (sometimes by coercion) to concentrate on
export-crops production and then sets itself up as
the sole authorized buyer of these export crops.
It buys them cheaply from the peasants and sells
them to the foreign importer at much higher prices
and retains the difference instead of passing it
on to the peasant producer. In this case the peasants
are self-employed but are nevertheless compelled
to submit to exploitation.

(iv) The examination of the relationship between the peasants and the government also implies that the present
problem of rural development, especially with respect
to food production cannot be solved within the existing political structures and relations of production
at large. The food and economic crisis facing most
African countries show that there is very little
potential for moving out of underdevelopment. The
policy makers themselves and the international organ-
izations such as the World Bank and the United Nations
agencies which inspire development strategies appear
to have run out of ideas. This is because they have
tried to 'solve the problems' within the context
of maintaining the existing relations of production
on the domestic and international level. The exhaustion of ideas is seen in the present attempts
in Tanzania to go back to development strategies

which were tried and discredited in the past. The
exhaustion of ideas is also illustrated by the report
set up by the United Nations to outline a new international development strategy for the 1980s. The
report '<u>Development in the 1980s: Approach to a New
Strategy</u>' (New York 1978) has no new strategy to
present. It just repeats familiar clichés such as
urging for "strengthening of institutions of international economic management".

BIBLIOGRAPHY

Ajjemi, A.H., Habari za Wakilindi, EALB, Nairobi 1972

Anderson-Morshead, A.E.M., The History of the UMCA 1857-1909, Vol. 1, London 1955

Ake, C., Explanatory Notes on the Political Economy of Africa, in Journal of Modern African Studies, 14, 1(1976)

Ake, C., Political Economy of Africa, Longman 1981

Allen, C., Unions, Income and Development, in Development Trends in Kenya, Edinburgh 1972

Alpers, E.A., The Coast and Development of Caravan Trade, in I. Kimambo and A. Temu, A History of Tanzania, Nairobi 1969

Arrighi, G., Essays on the Political Economy of Africa, New York, Monthly Review Press, 1973

Arrighi, G., International Corporations, Labour Aristocracies and Economic Development in Tropical Africa, in R.I. Rhodes (ed.), Imperialism and Underdevelopment, Monthly Review Press, 1970

Anshel-Russel, K.B. Agricultural Cooperatives and Markets in Developing Countries, New York 1969

Akpan, M.B. The African Policy of the Liberian Settlers, 1841-1930, A Study in the Native Policy of a Non-Colonial Power in Africa, Ibadan, Ph.D. Thesis 1968

Amin, S., Capitalism and Groundrent: The Domination of Capitalism over Agriculture in Tropical Africa, Dakar 1974

Bowles, B.D., The Political Economy of Tanganyika, Dar es salaam 1975

Brokensha, D., Handeni Revisited, in African Affairs, Vol. 70, No. 279, April 1970

Berg, E., Major Issues of Policy in Africa, in A.M. Rose (ed.), Industrial Relations and Economic Development, London 1966

Boesch, E.E., Kultur und Biotop, Saarbrücken 1975

Braundi, E.R., Neo-Colonialism and Class Struggle, International Journal 1, January 1964

Baxter, H.C., Religious Practices of the Pagan Wazigua, in TNR, 15, 1954

Bernstein, H., Concepts for the Analysis of Contemporary Peasantries, in Journal of Peasant Studies, 6, 4 (1979)

Braginskij, M.I., Die Herausbildung des Proletariats in Tropisch-Afrika, in Klaus Ernst and Leonid D. Jablockov, Afrika, Gegenwärtige soziale Prozesse und Strukturen, Verlag Berlin 1976

Baumann, O., Usambara und seine Nachbargebiete, Berlin 1891

Beidelmann, T.O., Matrilineal Peoples of Eastern Tanzania, London, IAI, 1967

Barthold, W.S., Farmers' Reaction to the Present Economic Situation in Tanzania: A Case Study of Five Villages in the Kilimanjaro Region, Berlin 1983

Coulson, A. (ed.), African Socialism in Practice, the Tanzania Experience, London 1979

Cabral, A., Revolution in Guinea Bissau, Monthly Review Press, New York 1969

Cliffe, L., Socialism in Tanzania, Vol. 2, Nairobi 1974

Couchman, F., Agricultural Change in Tanzania, Stanford Food Research Institute, 1970

Carter, G.M., African Studies in the United States, 1955-1975, New York 1977

Cleave, J.H., The African Farmers: Labour Use in the Development of Smallholder Agriculture, New York 1974

Connel, J., The Evolution of Tanzanian Rural Development, Dar es salaam 1976

Chodak, S., Social Stratification in Sub-Saharan Africa, in Journal of African Studies, 7(1973)

Deere, C.D., Rural Women's Subsistence Production in the Capitalist Periphery Economies, New York 1975

Doke, C.M., Bantu Modern Grammatic Phonetical and Lexicographical Studies since 1860, IAI, 1967

Daily News, 20.10.1974, 20.02.1976 and 19.03.1976

De Wilde, J.C., Experiences with Agricultural Development in Tropical Africa, Vol. 1, Baltimore, John Hopkins University Press, 1977

Dumont, R., Tanzania Agriculture after the Arusha Declaration, Dar es salaam, Government Printer 1969

Eggert, J., Missionsschule und sozialer Wandel in Ostafrika, Bertelsmann Universitätsverlag, Bd. 10, 1970

Elkan, W., Migrants and Proletarians, in G. Arrighi and J. Saul, Nationalism and Revolution in Sub-Saharan Africa, The Socialist Register, Monthly Review Press, 1960

Frank, A.G. Development of Underdevelopment, Monthly Review Press, New York 1966

Freedman, D., A Multi-Purpose Household Questionnaire, Washington D.C. 1977

Fanon, F., The Wretched of the Earth, Penguin 1963

Freire, P., Padagogy of the Oppressed, Herder and Herder 1970

Feierman, S., the Shambaa Kingdom. A History, Wisconsin 1974

Friedland, W.H., African Socialism, Stanford University Press 1974

Geertz, C., Agricultural Involution: The Process of Ecological Change, Berkeley, University of California Press, 1963

Goodard, D., Limits of British Anthropology, New Left Review, 58 (1969)

Gerken, E., Arbeitsmärkte in Entwicklungsländern, Kieler Studien, 163(1981)

Grohs, E., Kisazi, Reiferiten der Mädchen bei den Zigua und Ngulu Ost-Tanzanias, Dietrich Reimer Verlag 1977

Government of Tanganyika, People's Plan, Dar es salaam 1962

Garger, K., Tangaland und die Kolonisation Deutsch-Ostafrika, Berlin 1898

Guruli, K., The Role of NUTA in the Struggle for Socialism and Self-Reliance, in G. Ruhumbika (ed.), Towards Ujamaa, Nairobi 1974

Green, R., Political Independence and the National Economy: Essay in the Political Economy of Decolonisation, New York 1975

Galli, R.E. (ed.), The Political Economy of Rural Development, New York 1981

Hitchcock, E.F., Notes on the Sisal Industry, Tanga 1967

Hill, F., Experiments with Public Sector-Peasantry: Agricultural Schemes and Class Formation in Africa, Boston 1976

Hyden, G., Efficiency versus Distribution in East African Cooperatives, Nairobi 1964

Hyden, G., Beyond Ujamaa in Tanzania, Berkeley, University of California Press, 1980

Heilleiner, G.K., Agricultural Marketing in Tanzania, Policies and Problems, Dar es salaam, ERB Paper, 68(1970)

Hirji, K.F., School Education and Underdevelopment in Tanzania, in Maji Maji, No. 12, Dar es salaam 1973

Hinchcliffe, K., Labour Aristocracy, A Norhtern Nigerian Case Study, in Journal of Modern African Studies, 12, 1(1974)

Hopkin, R.F., Socialism and Participation. Tanzania's 1970 National Elections, Dar es salaam 1972

Hodgkin, T., Where the Paths Began, London 1976

Harlow, V., History of East Africa, Vol. II, Oxford University Press 1973

Ingle, C., From Village to State in Tanzania, The Politics of Development, Ithaca, Cornell University Press, 1972

Ibbot, G., Rural Development Programs in Tanzania: The Case of Ruvuma Region, Dar es salaam 1970

ILO, Unemployment and Structural Change, Geneva 1962

ILO, Meeting of Experts on Measurement of Underdevelopment, Working Paper No. 1, Geneva 1973

International Bank of Reconstruction and Development, The Economic Development of Tanganyika, Baltimore 1961

Illife, J., Tanzania under German Rule, Dar es salaam 1975

Illife, J., The Creation of Group Consciousness among the Dockworkers of Dar es salaam, 1929-1950, in Cohen, Robin, The Development of an African Working Class, Longman 1975

Knight, C.G. (ed.), Contemporary Africa, Geography and Change, New Jersey: Prentice Hill, 1976

Kerr, C., Industrialism of Labour and Management in Economic Growth, 2nd Edition, Oxford University Press, 1964

Kjekjus, H., The Question Hour in Tanzania Bunge, Dar es salaam 1972

Kaya, H.O., Effectiveness of the Existing Sisal-Based Industries in Reducing the Market Dependence of the Sisal Industry of Tanzania: A Case Study of the Tanga Region Industries, Dar es salaam 1978

Kaduma, I.M., Twenty Years of TANU Education, in Ruhumbika, G (ed.), Towards Ujamaa, Twenty Years of TANU Leadership, 1974

Kopytoff, I., Socialism and Traditional African Societies, Dar es salaam 1975

Kouter, J.H., Facts anf Factors in Rural Economy of the Nyakyusa in Tanzania, Leiden 1974

Kajumba, N., Socio-Economic Aspects of an African Plantation System: Tanzania Sisal Plantation Case, Dar es salaam 1977

Kartes, R.W., Twelve New Settlements in Tanzania, Dar es salaam 1969

Leys, C., Underdevelopment in Kenya, London 1975

Leonard, D.K., Reaching the Peasant Farmer, Chicago, University of Chicago Press, 1977

Lofchie, F.M., Agricultural Crisis and Economic Liberalism in Tanzania, Los Angeles 1975

Liebenow, J., Colonial Rule and Political Development in Tanzania: The Case Study of Makonde, Evanston, North-Western University Press, 1971

Lawrence, P.C., Plantation Sisal. The Inherited Mode of Production, in Cliffe, L. (ed.), Rural Cooperation in Tanzania, Tanzania Publishing House, Dar es salaam 1974

Lawrence, P.C., The Sisal Industry of Tanzania: A Review of the Informal Commodity Agreement and Related Questions of Strategy, ERB Paper 71.9, 1971

Lloyd, P.C., The New Elite of Tropical Africa, Oxford University Press 1966

Ledda, R., Social Classes and Political Struggle, in: International Socialist Journal, 1(22)1967

Lele, U., The Design of Rural Development, Lessons from Africa, Baltimore 1975

Lenin, V.I., Collected Works, Vol. 29, Moscow 1974

Lewis, W.A., Economic Development with Unlimited Supply of Labour, The Manchester School 1956

Mascarenhas, A.C., Resistance and Change in the Sisal Plantation System of Tanzania, Los Angeles, University of California, Ph.D. Thesis (Unpublished), 1970

Mokiva, A., Habari za Wazigua, London 1954

MacHenry, D.E. (Jr.), Policy Implementation in Rural Tanzania - Ujamaa Village, Dar es salaam 1975

Macpherson, G., Village Technology for Rural Development, Agricultural Innovation in Tanzania, Dar es salaam 1976

Murdock, G.P., Africa - Its Peoples and Their Culture, New York 1959

Mapolu, H., Agricultural Cooperation and Development of the Productive Forces: Some Lessons from Tanzania, in African Development, Vol. 1, No. 1, Dakar 1976

Mapolu, H., The Organisation and Participation of the Workers in Tanzania, in Journal of African Development and International Affairs, vol. 2, 3(1973)

Menzel, H. (ed.), The Relationship Between Individual and Collective Properties, New York 1970

Mitchell, J.C., Occupational Prestige and Social Status, Africa, New York, 29(1969)

Marshall, J., The State of Ambivalence: Right and Left Options in Ghana, Review of African Political Economy, 1974

Mellor, J.W., Agricultural Price Policy and Income Distribution in Africa, Washington, D.C., 1973

Marx, K., Capital, Vol. 1, Moscow 1972

Marx, K., and F. Engels, Manifesto of the Communist Party, in Selected Works, Moscow 1975

Mamdani, M., Politics and Class Formation in Uganda, New York, Monthly Review Press, 1976

Mathias, R., The Falling of Educational Standards in Primary Schools in Tanzania, University of Dar es salaam, Department of Education, 1977

Mushi, S.S., Ujamaa: Modernisation by Traditionalisation, in Taamuli, 12(1972)

McVicar, T., Wanguru, Religions, in Primitive Man, 1, 1939

McVicar, T., The Relations between Religion and Morality Among the Wazigua, in Primitive Man, 1, 1939

Maunder, W.F., Employment in an Underdeveloped Area, New Haven, Yale University² Press, 1972

Marketing Development Bureau, Large Scale Maize Production, Ministry of Agriculture, DSM, 1976

Norman, D.W., the Organisational Consequences of Social and Economic Constraints and Policies in Dry-Land Areas, Reading 1974

Nyerere, J.K., Socialism and Rural Development, in Freedom and Development, Oxford University Press 1974

Nyerere, J.K., The Arusha Declaration, Ten Years After, Dar es salaam 1977

Nyerere, J.K., New Year Speech on Adult Education, Dar es salaam 1969

Neil, J., Economy and Society: A Study in Integration of Economic and Social Theory, Boston 1975

Payne, G., Sociology and Social Research, London 1981

Porter, P.W., Climate and Agriculture in Africa, New Jersey 1976

Rodney, W., How Europe Underdeveloped Africa, Dar es salaam 1972

RKA, No. 120

Raum, O.F., German East Africa: Changes in African Life under German Administration, 1892-1914, in Harlow, V., History of East Africa, Vol. III, Oxford University Press, 1965

Rweyemamu, J., Underdevelopment and Industrialization in Tanzania, A Study of Perverse Industrial Development, Oxford University Press, 1973

Sagarin, E. (ed.), Sociology, The Basic Concepts, New York 1978

Sprinsak, E., African Traditional Socialism, in Journal of Modern African Studies, 2, 4(1973)

Safa, H.I., Class Consciousness Among Working Class Women in Capitalist Periphery, in Ray Bromley and Chris Gerry (eds.), Casual Work and Poverty in the Third World, New York 1975

Schönmeier, H.W., Agriculture in Conflict - The Shambaa Case, Kübel Foundation, Bensheim 1977

Shivji, I.G., Tanzania: The Class Struggle Continues, Dar es salaam 1973

Saul, J., and Woods, R., African Peasantry, Longman 1981

Storch, L., Sitten, Gebräuche und Rechtspflege bei Bewohnern Usambaras, Berlin 1895

Silberfein, M., African Cultivator, A Geographical Overview, Crossroads Pres 1978

Sandbrook, R., The Development of an African Working Class: Studies in Class Formation and Action, London 1975

Schram, S.R., *The Political Thought of Mao Tse-Tung*, New York 1963

Stichter, S., *The Formation of a Working Class in Kenya*, in Sandbrook, R. (ed.), *African Working Class*, London 1975

Shanin, T., *Peasants and Peasant Societies*, Penguin Books 1971

Szentes, T., *The Political Economy of Underdevelopment*, Budapest 1975

Tanzania Sisal Authority, *Annual Labour Reports*, Tanga 1980

TIRDEP, *Tanga Regional Development Plan, 1975-1980*, Tanga 1975

Tanganyika Government, *Annual Report of the Provincial Commissioner*, Tanga 1939

Tanganyika Government, *Annual Report of the Labour Department*, Dar es salaam, Government Printer, 1944

Tanganyika Territory Government, *Annual Medical Report*, Dar es salaam, Government Printer, 1924

TANU, *Party Guidelines*, Dar es salaam 1972

Temu, A., *Public Involvement in Planning and Development in Tanzania*, University of York, Overseas School, 1973

Tambila, A., *A History of the Tanga Sisal Labour Force, 1939-1964*, University of Dar es salaam, M.A. Thesis (Unpublished), 1974

United Republic of Tanzania Government, *The Village and Ujamaa Villages Registration, Designation and Administration Act*, Dar es salaam 1975

United Nations Economic Commission for Africa (UNECA), Human Resource Development Division, *Women: The Neglected Human Resource for African Development*, in Canadian Journal of African Studies, Vol. 6, 2(1972)

UNO Paper, E/CN.24/CAP.6/2

United Republic of Tanzania Government, *Second Five Year Plan for Economic and Social Development*, Vol. 1, Dar es salaam 1974

United Republic of Tanzania Government, Election Study Committee, Socialism and Participation, Dar es salaam 1975

von Freyhold, M., The Potentials for Ujamaa in Handeni: Some Ecological and Historical Characteristics of the District, Dar es salaam 1972

von Freyhold, M., Ujamaa Villages in Tanzania, An Analysis of a Social Experiment, London 1979

von Freyhold, M., The Formation of the Class of Wage-labourers in Tanzania under Colonial Capitalism, Dar es salaam 1975

von Velzen, H.U.E.T., Staff Kulaks and Peasants, Nairobi 1974

Warner, U., Formulating Guidelines for Rural Water Investment: The Case Study of Tanzania, Dar es salaam 1976

Waterman, P., The Concept of 'Semi-Proletarianized' Peasantry, An Empirical and Theoretical Note, The Hague, Labour Study Group 1979

Westergaard, P., Farm Surveys of Cashew Producers in Mtwara Region, Univerity of Dar es salaam, ERB Paper 71.9 (1971)

Weisner, T., One Family, Two Households: A Rural-Urban Network Model of Urbanism, Nairobi 1978

Williams, G., The Social Stratification of an Neo-Colonial Economy, Western Nigeria, in Allen, C. (ed.), African Perspectives, Cambridge University Press 1970

Wolf, E., Peasants, New Jersey 1966

World Bank, The Economic Development of Tanganyika, Baltimore 1961

APPENDIX

APPENDIX I

Topic: The Problems of Regional Development in Tanzania:
A Case Study of the Tanga Region

Questionaire Ia:
Village Survey   Date:_____

District:_____   Division:_____

General Information:

1. Name of Village   : _____
2. Type of Village   : _____
3. Name of Village Chairman   : _____
4. Name of Village Secretary   : _____
5. Number of Cells (End of 1982): _____
6. Number of Households (End of 1982): _____
7. Age Groups in 1982   : _____

	Below 15 Years	15-50 Years	Over 50 Years
Male			
Female			
Total			

8. Village History

a) Meaning of the Village Name:_____
b) Date and Circumstances of Village Formation:_____

_____

9. **Housing Patterns (Types of Houses)**

			More than 50%	10-50%
a)	Clay with Traditional Roof	:	_____	_____
b)	Clay with Iron Roof	:	_____	_____
c)	Bricks with Iron Roof	:	_____	_____

d) Other Buildings beside Main House:

Kitchen: _-_____   Latrine:_____   Store-house:_____

Others : _____

10. **Socio-economic Facilities:**

a) School (primary)   : _____
b) School (secondary) : _____
c) Church   : _____
d) Mosque   : _____
e) Dispensary   : _____
f) Cooperative Shops   : _____
g) Private Shops   : _____
h) Market Place   : _____
i) CCM-Office   : _____
j) UWT-Office/Branch   : _____
k) Water Supply   : _____ (Type)_____

   Distance from Village:_____
   Number of Wells/Taps :_____
   Condition of Supply :_____
   Seasonal Changes of Water Supply:_____
   Other Sources of Water Supply and their Conditions:_____

11. **Accessibility of the Village:**

a) Distance to the next Village:_____

Distance to District Headquarters:_____

b) Accessibility by Car in:

J	F	M	A	M	J	J	A	S	O	N	D

c) Public Transport Facilities:

Means	Destination	Frequency	Fare
Bus	_____	_____	____
Others	_____	_____	____

d) Private Means of Transport Available in the Village:

Bicycles:_____ Motorcycles:_____

Tractors, Pick-up Trucks, Lorries:-_____

Others : _____

e) Public Communication Facilities:

Telephones:_____

Telegraphs:_____

Others : _____

12. **Migration:**

a) Are there Villagers regularly working outside the Village?

Male:_____ Female:_____ Total:_____

b) Where do they mostly look for Employment?_____

c) Are People from outside regulary coming to the Village for Work?

Male:_____ Female:_____ Total:_____

13. **Village Economy:**

a) Are any of the following Activities performed by People in the Village?

Blacksmith   : _____

Carpentry   : _____

Pottery   : _____

Basket Making: _____

b) Do you have a Communal Plot? Yes_____ No_____

   Size   : _____(acres)

   Distance from Village: _____(km)

   Organisation of Work : _____(e.g. every family working there once a week, or some few people doing all the work)

c) Average Size of Farm in this Village? _____(acres)

d) Which Crop occupies the largest Part of the cultivated Land in the Village? _____

e) Basic Staple Food in the Village:

   Cassava _____   Maize _____   Millet/Sorghum _____

   Rice   _____

   Others _____

f) Do the Villagers produce enough Staple Food for Home Consumption or do they have to by additional Food from outside the Village?

   Yes _____ No _____

   If yes, what kind of food is bought? _____

g) Animal Husbandry:

   How many Families have:

	More than 50%	10-50%
Poultry		
Goats, Sheep		
Cattle		

14. **Marketing:**

a) What is the most important Crop for getting Cash Money?_____

b) To whom is this Crop sold?

   Consumers_____ Traders_____ Cooperatives_____

   State Coporation_____

c) Which other agricultural Crop is sold?_____

d) What is the most important non-agricultural Product sold by the Villagers?_____

e) Where is this Product sold?

   Within the Village?_____

   Outside the Village?_____

f) Main Problems facing the Villagers in the Marketing of their Produce?_____

   _____

   _____

15. **Socio-Economic Development:**

a) Credit:

   Did the Village or Groups inside the Village receive or try to receive any Credit/Loan in the Past?

   Yes_____ No_____

   For what Purpose?_____

   Terms of Credit ?_____

b) <u>Development Programmes:</u>

   Since Independence, what kind of Development Programmes have been carried out/initiated in the Village?_____

   _____

Who initiated these Projects?_____

Financing of the Projects?   _____

Results: _____

Most important Projects the Villagers wish to carry out in the Future?_____

APPENDIX II

Questionaire Ib

Household Interviews   Date:_____

Village:_____   District:_____   Division:_____

Name of Head of Household:_____

Cell-Leader   :_____

1. I would like to know how many people usually live here and eat together in this household, counting all adults, children and infants?

Name	Relationship to Head of Household	Age	Sex

2. Just to make sure I have a complete listing. Are there any persons who usually lived here and ate with you during the past year but are temporarily away for some reason?_____

3. Employment and Migration Modules:

   Have you been working:

a) as unpaid Family Labour (after the age of 15 years)_____(years)

b) as paid(Migratory)Worker?_____

   Place:_____

   Kind of Work:_____

c) Self-employed outside the Village_____(years)

Place: _____

Kind of Work: _____

d) On your Farm: _____(years)

e) Do you have any official Function in the Village: Yes__ No__

If yes, which: _____

f) Which kind of Activities do you and other Members of your Household do beside agricultural Work?

Kind of Activity	Employer (for whom)	Season	For Sale	Price/Income

g) Do you or any Member of your Household do unpaid Work including communal Activities?

Person	Kind of Work	For whom	Time/Frequency	Reason

4. **Land Ownership, Location and Use**

a) How many Farms do you have?

Number of Farms: _____

Yours: _____

Belonging to other Members of Household: _____

b) Where are these Farms located and how do you use them?

Farm	Location	Size(acres)	Main Crops	Other Crops

c) How did you aquire your Farm?

Inherited:_____

Bought:_____

Right of Occupancy by Village Council:_____

Other Means:_____

d) Besides these Farms, do you have additional Land(outside the village)?

Yes_____   No_____

If yes, how many acres?_____(acres)

e) How many of your Farms are currently not in Use?_____

Why_____

f) Is there any Possibility for you to aquire new Land?_____

5. <u>Animal Husbandry:</u>

a) Do you keep any Animals?

Type of Animals	Number	Method of Keeping				Purpose				
		Tied	Loose	Fenced	Stable	Milk	Meat	Eggs	Draft	Other

e) Do you intend to expand your Animal Enterprise? Yes__ No__

   If Yes:Why:_____

          How:_____

6. <u>Labour Utilization:</u>

a) Which is the busiest Month for you during the Year?_____

b) What kind of Work is done at this Time?_____

c) Which Crops do you start with in your agricultural Work at this Time?_____

d) Is your Household Labour Capacity sufficient for all your agricultural work?_____

7. <u>Inputs:</u>

a) Do you by any Inputs like Seeds, Fertilizer, Chemicals,etc.

   Yes_____ No_____

   If yes, which are these?

Input	Amount	Expenses	Purpose

b) How is the Supply of Fertilizers and Chemicals?

   Regular:_____   Irregular:_____   Sufficient:_____

   Insufficient:_____   (Not) in Time:_____

c) Which Equipment do you use on your Farm?

Type of Equipment	Quantity	Price(if bought)	Charge(if rented)
Hoe			
Cutlass			
Axe			

Plough			
Tractor			
Others			

d) What Possibilities do you have to get a Credit? _____

e) What are the Conditions?

Purpose	From Whom	Duration	Interest Rate	Repayment

f) If you want to expand or modernize your Farm, what would be the most important Help to you? _____

8. Income and Expenditure:

a) How much do you harvest from each Crop per Year? _____
b) Do you process any Product before selling? _____

Crop	Total Harvest	Own Consumption	For Sale	Sold To

c) Which recurrent Expenses do you have for the Household?

Item	Amount	Time/Frequency

d) Do you sometimes have to buy Stable Food that you produce on your farm?

Kind of Food	Season	Amount	Price	Where bought

e) Reasons:_____
_____

f) Is there any Money left from your Household's Income at the End of the Year?_____
How much?_____
What do you use it for?_____

SPEKTRUM
Berliner Reihe zu Gesellschaft, Wirtschaft und
Politik in Entwicklungsländern · ISSN 0176-277 X

Herausgegeben von
Prof. Dr. Volker Lühr und Prof. Dr. Manfred Schulz
Freie Universität Berlin · Institut für Soziologie
Babelsberger Straße 14-16 · 1000 Berlin 31

---

1 Uta Borges et al., Proalcool: Analyse und Evaluierung des brasilianischen Biotreibstoffprogramms. 1984. V, 226 S. ISBN 3-88156-265-6.

2 Helmut Asche (Hrsg.), Dritte Welt für Journalisten: Zwischenbilanz eines Weiterbildungsangebotes. 1984. 231 S. ISBN 3-88156-266-4.

3 Detlev Ullrich, Barriopolitik in Caracas (Venezuela): eine sozialempirische Untersuchung am Beispiel der Erwachsenenbildung und der Stadtteilarbeit. 1984. XI, 388 S. Zahlr. Fotos, Schaub., Tab. ISBN 3-88156-280-X.

4 Thomas Hurtienne: Theoriegeschichtliche Grundlagen des sozialökonomischen Entwicklungsdenkens. 1984. Bd.I: Rationalität und sozialökonomische Entwicklung in der frühbürgerlichen Epoche. XVI, 264 S. Bd. II: Paradigmen sozialökonomischer Entwicklung im 19. und 20. Jahrhundert. V, 422 S. ISBN 3-88156-285-0.

5 Volker Lühr (Hrsg.): Die Dritte Welt vor der Tür? Zwischen christlichem Wohlfahrtskonzern und türkischem Frauenladen: Berichte über Projekte der »Selbsthilfe« in Berlin. 1984. 216 S. ISBN 3-88156-292-3.

6 Wolfram Kühn: Agrarreform und Agrarkooperativen in Nicaragua. 1985. IV, 131 S. ISBN 3-88156-299-0.

7 Hassan Omari Kaya: Problems of Regional Development in Tanzania. 1985. VII, 243 S. ISBN 3-88156-302-4.

Verlag **breitenbach** Publishers
Memeler Straße 50, D-6600 Saarbrücken, Germany
P.O.B. 16243 Fort Lauderdale, Fla. 33318, USA